KU-394-655

Gardening in the Shade

I. F. la Croix
Illustrated by the author

Angus & Robertson
Publishers

Acknowledgements

I should like to thank the following: my husband, for taking some of the photographs and designing the garden layouts;
Mr Arthur Headlam; Mrs Sheila Robley; Mrs Jean Hughes.

ANGUS & ROBERTSON · PUBLISHERS
Brighton · Sydney · Melbourne · Singapore · Manila

This book is copyright. Apart from any fair
dealing for the purposes of private study,
research, criticism or review, as permitted
under the Copyright Act, no part may be
reproduced by any process without written
permission. Inquiries should be addressed
to the publisher.

First published by Angus & Robertson (UK) Ltd,
16 Ship Street, Brighton, Sussex, in 1978

Copyright © I.F. la Croix 1978

ISBN 0 207 95752 5

Set in 10 on 12pt Ehrhardt 453 by
HBM Typesetting Ltd, Standish Street,
Chorley, Lancashire

Printed photolitho in Great Britain by
Ebenezer Baylis & Son Ltd., The Trinity Press,
Worcester, and London

Contents

Colour Illustrations

Introduction

No garden has perfect conditions, certainly not for growing all kinds of plants. It is important to assess what your garden has to offer, and to approach any problem in as positive a way as possible. Sometimes corrective action is obvious and relatively easy to take—for example, in a windswept garden, it is essential to plant resistant species as windbreaks. It is surprising, however, how often a so-called problem can be turned into an asset by considering the advantages of a site rather than the drawbacks, and by selecting plants suited to these particular conditions.

In a shaded garden, one cannot hope to grow sun-loving plants, but many of the most beautiful of garden plants, such as rhododendrons, camellias and primulas, thrive in shady conditions. Also, a shaded garden is very likely to be a sheltered one, which is a considerable asset.

Shade, of course, is not a blanket term—there is dry shade and damp shade, and the plants one would choose for these situations would be very different. Again, the conditions that prevail in a woodland garden are different from those in a town garden, where the shade is usually caused by buildings rather than trees.

One does not need to have a garden that is entirely shaded to be interested in this subject. Most gardens have some shaded areas and if the best can be made of these, it adds greatly to the variety and therefore to the interest of the garden. I hope in this book to suggest ways to make the most of all sorts of shaded garden.

I

The Nature of the Problem

It is difficult to imagine a garden with no shade; after all, almost every house has a wall that gets little or no sun. The word 'shade' means the cutting out of light, and as far as a garden is concerned, this can happen in basically two ways: by the presence of an overhead canopy, that is to say branches, or by the effect of some structure which cuts out direct sunlight but leaves the area in question open to the sky above. This is an important distinction, as there are many plants which grow well in the second situation, but not the first.

The first category is represented by the woodland garden—in its most reduced form, as one or two trees. Trees, of course, cast their shade over a much greater area than that directly beneath their branches, and so even a single large tree growing on the sunny side of a garden can exert a considerable influence on conditions in that garden. In a case like this, the most obvious solution might seem to be to cut down the tree, but this may not be possible or desirable for a number of reasons. Ideally, large forest trees that are able to shade an entire garden, or a large part of it, should not be grown near houses, but many are, and have to be accepted as *faits accomplis*.

The second category of shade is most likely to be found in town gardens, where there are tall buildings all around. Some shade of this type is found in almost all gardens and very often the dark side of a house is more or less a wasted area—used perhaps for dustbins, wood-piles or coal bunkers, but wasted from a gardening point of view. This is a pity, as few gardens are so extensive that the owner can afford to lose part of it.

Each type of shade exists in varying degrees. In permanent shade, the sun does not reach the ground at all. This, of course, gives the least choice of plants able to grow there. In partial shade, the sun reaches the area in question for some time each day. Obviously there is a point where partial shade occurs for so short a time that it can be disregarded for practical purposes. In this book, we are dealing with situations where the plant is shaded for the greater part of the day. The time of day that the area is in shade is important—in a hot climate, it is much more useful if the sun is cut off in the middle of the day. Morning shade can be useful as well. Most authorities consider that early-flowering plants, such as camellias, can have their flowers damaged by too rapid a thaw if they have been slightly frozen during the night. I must say that I have not noticed this effect myself—in our garden, flowers seem either to be completely browned by frost, or are not

I

affected, and whether they get sun first thing in the morning or not seems quite irrelevant. However, the proviso is so widely quoted that I feel there must be some truth in it.

Shade, of course, changes with the seasons; as the sun mounts higher in the sky, the amount becomes less. This is something it can be difficult to visualise at another time of year. In a new garden it is advisable not to be in too much of a hurry to put in permanent plantings, so as to see how much shade different parts of the garden get at different times of year. Woodland, too—at least deciduous woodland—has its own seasonal aspect. Even where shade is dense in summer, quite a lot of light may reach the ground in spring.

Dappled shade occurs where the sun is filtered through branches but is not completely cut out. Many plants grow particularly well in this situation.

Within these categories, one can make a further sub-division into dry and damp shade. The latter is much easier to cope with but the former, unfortunately, is more common. This is because the feature that causes the shade—for example a high wall—often has also a rain-shadow effect. If the shade is caused by a tree, there is also competition for water by its roots.

These areas of dry shade can be improved to some extent. As much humus as possible should be dug in so that the soil will be better able to hold moisture. Peat, leaf-mould and garden compost are all suitable. Any plants growing there should be mulched, making sure that the soil is damp first. A mulch slows down the rate of evaporation from the soil, but it also helps to stop rain from soaking through. If this does not have sufficient effect, the answer is to grow those plants that can cope with dry shade—there are not a great many, but there are some, which are listed in the Appendix.

Shade is not necessarily static. As well as the seasonal changes mentioned earlier, there is the fact that plants grow. The shade in mature woodland or in a town garden where the shade comes from buildings may change little from year to year, but in a recently planted garden, there will be considerable changes as trees and shrubs develop, and what was originally a sunny position can eventually become a shaded one. Again, the extent to which this will happen can be difficult to visualise, but it can be allowed for by not making permanent plantings in situations where it is obvious that there is going to be a change in the course of a few years. This does not mean one has to stick to annuals and biennials, useful though they may be in such circumstances. Quite a few sun-loving shrubs and sub-shrubs are naturally shortlived and easily propagated, such as helianthemums, tree lupins and the various members of the genus *Cistus*. These can be used for a few years and the planting changed later. There is no need to hurry over this. We had a specimen of *Cistus creticus* that grew and flowered for several years after its originally sunny position had become quite heavily shaded.

Shade is often thought of as a drawback in, for example, the British Isles, where sun is usually in short supply; but in countries where the summer at least is habitually hot, the value of shade is appreciated and gardens are often planned with this in mind. Shade, however, has its advantages in any climate—shade implies shelter, for one thing. A light canopy of branches is sometimes sufficient to keep off a light frost, and plants such as early rhododendrons growing in that situation may escape damage to the flowers where those in a more open site are caught by frost. It is also worth growing these early flowerers in front of a shaded wall. In such a position, flowering is often retarded by a couple of weeks which may be enough to allow the blooms to escape the period when frost is most likely to occur. I am talking here about species such as *Rhododendron pemakoense* and *R. × praecox*, which are perfectly hardy in themselves, but flower in early spring. The flower-buds are hardy until they swell up just before opening and it is then and when the flowers are open that frost is so damaging.

Town gardens have a further advantage in that the winter temperature is often slightly higher than that of the surrounding countryside, and so plants that are considered doubtfully hardy in that general area may survive without damage.

Wind, whether hot and dry or cold and blustery, is one of the worst enemies of plants, and both woodland-type and town gardens are likely to be relatively protected from that. One problem that can arise in a town garden, however, is that of a wind-tunnel effect, when wind seems to become funnelled down passages and round corners of buildings. This can be very damaging, although often the effect is confined to quite a limited area. If this happens, it is usually possible to fit up some sort of screen or trellis, or plant some particularly wind-resistant shrub to break its force. A solid barrier is never as satisfactory a windbreak as a broken one, such as a hedge or trellis. The former diverts the wind upwards and causes turbulence some distance away, while the latter filters it and reduces its force.

Another useful 'side-effect' of shade is that flowers usually last longer and keep their colour better than in full sun. Some colours seem more liable to fade than others—orange and salmon particularly. The flowers of *Rhododendron kaempferi*, an evergreen species of the azalea series, and its many hybrids such as the brick-red 'John Cairns', lose colour very quickly in the hot sun, as do those of the hybrid rhododendron 'Fabia' and *Potentilla* 'Tangerine'.

Some plants must have shade and others will grow in either sun or shade. Others again, although they do not concern us here, must have a position in full sun. Is there any physiological difference between these 'sun' and 'shade' plants? Certain plants are adapted for living in conditions of low light intensity. The most extreme examples are those which no longer live like plants, but have lost their chlorophyll and become either parasites, like toothwort and the broomrapes, or saprophytes like the bird's nest orchid. This last, *Neottia nidus-avis,* is a British native found in beechwoods, particularly on chalk. There are no leaves; all that is visible above ground are the flower-stalks and flowers. The whole plant is a pale brown, just slightly lighter in tone than the brown of the dead leaves that cover the ground and upon which it lives. The roots form a close association with a fungus and it is this that breaks down the dead leaves and obtains the food upon which it and the orchid live. By being adapted in this way to conditions of very low light intensity, the bird's nest orchid is able to live virtually free from the competition of other plants.

Parasites live on other plants, often on the roots, so that they appear to be growing independently from the ground. Total parasites again have no chlorophyll. There are a number of species like this, often mauve or reddish-brown in colour, but they are rarely plentiful. Almost all are specific to one or a very few species of host plant, which must limit their spread. I have sometimes seen one of these growing in gardens, namely *Lathraea clandestina,* a native of mainland Europe, which, according to the textbooks, parasitises the roots of willow and poplar, but which I have also seen growing on maples and rhododendrons. It has showy violet flowers in spring, and would be well worth growing if possible. To begin with, there would have to be a suitable host plant growing in the garden. It is not easy to get the parasite established, even if it can be obtained, as it has no roots as such—it grows into the host so that the conducting tissues are continuous. However, I am told it can be done by cutting out a piece of root with the parasite attached and inserting this in the soil beside a root of the new host. It is also sometimes successful to scatter seed near the trunk of a suitable host.

Lathraea squamaria, Toothwort, is a related species that is parasitic on hazel and elm and is found wild in the British Isles, Europe and the Himalayas. It has curious pale violet-mauve flowers, but is much less showy than the previous species. If it were possible to establish any of these plants in a garden, they would certainly grow in dense shade, but I fear they must remain curiosities rather than practical propositions for most people, as I do not know of any commercial sources. These plants are small and would be unlikely to cause any damage to the host unless the latter was very small and the colony of parasites very large.

Except for such unusual species, all plants need some light to survive, as it is by the use of light energy in the presence of the green pigment chlorophyll that they are able to manufacture sugars by photosynthesis. Each plant needs a minimum amount of light in order to survive, but this amount can differ considerably from one species to another. 'Shade plants' are able to photosynthesise at lower light intensities than most other plants, and they also reach maximum production at a lower intensity. Any extra light cannot be used, and the leaves may become scorched.

One simple adaptation to life in the shade is that used by many common woodland plants such as the wood anemone and wood sorrel. By flowering early in the year, the part of their life cycle with the greatest energy requirement, that is, flowering and seed formation, is completed before the canopy of leaves develops.

Some plants seem relatively indifferent to the amount of light received, for example *Choisya ternata,* the Mexican Orange. We grow this in a border where it gets full sun for the whole day, and it grows and flowers freely. It also grows well in quite heavily shaded situations, although possibly flowering less freely. A plant grown in shade often has a quite different appearance from the same variety grown in sun—the leaves are larger and softer, and growth is taller and laxer.

Apart from those at either extreme, there is no way of saying in absolute terms how much shade a particular type of plant should have. Some, like the Kurume azaleas, that need a fair bit of shade even in southern England, let alone Australia or the United States, need full sun in Scotland, otherwise the wood does not ripen sufficiently for flower-buds to develop. Cultivars of *Camellia japonica* are in the same category—the *williamsii* hybrids are much more free-flowering than the *japonicas* in Scotland and other areas where the intensity of sun is low. In general, the hotter the sun, the more shade a plant is likely to require, but amounts of water available also seem to have some influence. Where there is a good supply of water, a plant can often tolerate more exposure than if the soil were dry.

How can one tell if a plant is wrongly sited and is receiving either too much sun or not enough? A shade plant grown in sun usually develops yellowish leaves, which may actually become scorched, and makes little growth. A sun-loving species situated in too dense a shade grows lax and floppy and 'out of character', and will flower poorly, if at all.

Plants with red or purple leaves do not usually do well in shade. This colouring is caused by pigments called anthocyanins which are dissolved in the cell sap and not contained in the chloroplasts as is chlorophyll. These pigments absorb light energy, but this is not available for photosynthesis and is released as heat. Because some light that might have been absorbed by the chloroplasts has been taken up by anthocyanins, the efficiency of photosynthesis at low light intensities is reduced. At high intensities, there is light to spare and the rate of photosynthesis is not affected. In practice, such plants tend to lose their reddish colouring if grown in too shady a place. *Ajuga reptans,* the Bugle, is a creeping plant that is a useful ground-cover in shade.

There are one or two varieties with bronze or purple leaves. We planted one of these, 'Burgundy Glow', under a quince tree and although the plants grew well enough, the attractive purple colouring almost disappeared. We moved them to a sunny position and the colour soon returned. Similarly, plants whose autumn colour is part of their attraction rarely develop this as well when grown in shade, and this should be kept in mind when siting them.

In a very gloomy area, variegated and golden-leaved plants are particularly effective, as they give the impression of sunlight striking the leaves. In dense shade, variegated plants are at some disadvantage, as only the green parts of the leaves can photosynthesise, but when the variegation is only to the extent of a white or yellow border to the leaf, as is often the case, this does not have too much effect. Many shade-tolerant plants have variegated cultivars and most of these can also cope with shady conditions as long as they do not have to compete with a vigorous, wholly green variety, when they would probably be choked out. Any all-green shoots that appear on a variegated plant should be cut out or these will increase at the expense of the original.

In areas where sunlight is intense, such as most of the United States and Australia, almost all variegated plants must be grown in at least partial shade or the leaves become scorched. This can also be a problem with golden-leaved plants. The golden-foliage form of the common flowering currant, *Ribes sanguineum* 'Brocklebankii', is a good example—even in England the leaves scorch in full sun. The same happens with the golden-leaved marjoram, *Origanum vulgare* 'Aureum', which can be used as a herb in cooking in the same way as the ordinary variety.

Obviously, evergreens with variegated or gold colouring are the most valuable, as their effect is present even in winter. Among shrubs, one of the best is the golden privet, *Ligustrum ovalifolium* 'Aureum', which can make a splash of yellow as vivid as a forsythia in full bloom. I have seen this growing well in shade, although if it is really dense, the colour is less bright. It is a very fine plant, especially when it is allowed to grow naturally and is not clipped hard. *Aucuba japonica* has a number of variegated forms (known generally as Spotted Laurels or Gold Dust plants) with the variegation usually taking the form of spots rather than the more common white or yellow edging. It is dioecious, that is, male and female flowers are borne on different plants, and if both male and female forms are planted, handsome red berries are produced on the latter. 'Gold Dust' and 'Variegata' are female cultivars and 'Crotonifolia' and 'Speckles' are male. In very dense shade, the variegation is less bright. Much less well known than this is *Camellia* × *williamsii* 'Golden Spangles', a cultivar whose leaves have a central yellowish blotch. The flowers are single pink.

Turning to ground-cover plants, there are variegated forms of both the greater and lesser periwinkle. *Vinca major* 'Maculata' has a yellowish blotch, again less marked in deep shade, but much more striking is 'Variegata', with a creamy-white border and blotches, and it is almost as vigorous as its green counterpart. *Vinca minor* has the cultivars 'Aureovariegata' and 'Variegata', with yellow and creamy-white markings respectively. Neither of these is quite as rampant as the green forms. *Pachysandra terminalis* has the variegated forms 'Variegata' and 'Silveredge'.

The variegated ivies, cultivars of *Hedera canariensis, H. colchica* and *H. helix,* are invaluable both as ground-covers and on a wall or fence. There are too many of them to mention here, but a list of variegated plants suitable for shade, both evergreen and deciduous, is given at the end of the book and fuller descriptions of individual species are given in the alphabetical listing of plants.

Among deciduous trees and shrubs with gold foliage, one of the best is the Golden Elder, *Sambucus nigra* 'Aurea'. It is hardy and grows on any soil, and has leaves of a really rich yellow. The golden form of the red-berried elder, *S. racemosa* 'Plumosa Aurea', is even more beautiful as the foliage is finely divided as well as being a lovely colour.

2

Planning the Garden

People make gardens for many different reasons, including such simple ones as providing a supply of cut flowers for the house, or preventing the neighbours complaining about weeds. However, most of those with sufficient interest in gardening to read a book about it must find that much of the satisfaction comes from attempting to grow plants as well as possible and perhaps in trying to make difficult plants flourish.

It is possible to achieve a very attractive effect by using quite ordinary plants, and only a few varieties of these, but this tends to be boring to live with. This type of planting seems more a branch of decorating than of horticulture. A garden is a three-dimensional picture which one walks into and through—smell and touch are important as well as sight. An element of variety and, if possible, surprise is to my mind essential.

It is, of course, all too easy to carry this approach to extremes and to have a garden that is full of plants that may be interesting as individuals, but have no coherence as a landscape. It is even more unfortunate to concentrate on difficult and unusual plants to such an extent that the garden is reminiscent of a horticultural convalescent home.

The most satisfactory approach combines the artistic and the plant-loving. There should be a preponderance of plants that are known to grow well in the locality; if they occupy the key positions, the more difficult species can be confined to a few favourable situations. Having said that, it is necessary to add that one should not confine oneself to plants that are growing in neighbours' gardens. In general, people's choice of plants tends to be conservative, and there are many perfectly easy and hardy plants that are seldom grown, sometimes for no discernible reason. In some cases, it may be simply that there is no common non-botanical name. Also, local garden centres tend to stock only those plants that are most frequently asked for, therefore these are the ones that people buy, and so a vicious circle is perpetuated. For more unusual plants, it will probably be necessary to go to specialist nurseries, but most of these will send plants by post if there is not one near at hand. Even with well-known plants, relatively few varieties are grown. One sees the double pink Japanese cherry known as Kanzan or Sekiyama over and over again; it is hardy and free-flowering certainly, yet so are many other varieties.

In a garden where one can grow almost anything, the choice of what to plant can be quite bewildering. One advantage of having some sort of limiting factor in a garden, such as shade, is that by cutting down choice it helps to concentrate the mind and produce a more coherent result. This is when it is helpful to have a positive attitude towards the limiting factor, whatever it might be, and to see it as an asset rather than a drawback. For example, rather than attempt to make a shaded garden a riot of colour, it is usually better to emphasise the cool and restful quality of shade. This does not mean that one should avoid colour altogether, or should not try to bring an effect of dappled sunlight into a dark corner by planting a variety with golden leaves, as already described.

The fashion now is for informal gardens, partly because tastes have changed and many people find formal styles stiff and forbidding, but mainly for economic reasons. Most people now do not have help in their gardens, or have less than they used to, and therefore need something that is easily looked after. Bedding plants are both expensive and labour-intensive, and so gardens tend to be planted mostly with trees and shrubs and ground-cover plants which, once established, require much less in the way of maintenance. This style is well suited to shady gardens, and the basic principles of design apply to these as to any others.

Any garden needs a permanent framework of woody plants. This applies as much to the room-size garden as to the big estate—the important thing is to make sure that trees and shrubs selected are in the right scale. A very small courtyard-type garden would probably not have any trees, unless perhaps dwarf conifers, but there are many dwarf shrubs that can be used in the smallest space, even in troughs or window-boxes.

A lawn is usually considered indispensable, but a very small garden, particularly one of the courtyard type, is better without one. Lawns are difficult anywhere in permanent shade, and particularly under trees. It is possible to buy special grass mixtures where sowing in the shade is unavoid-able. In Britain, these mixtures are usually based on perennial ryegrass (*Lolium perenne*) or *Agrostis stolonifera*, relatively coarse perhaps, but hard-wearing and pretty shade-tolerant.

There is currently quite a lot of interest in the use of plants other than grass for making lawns, the main purpose of this being to avoid mowing. I have no personal experience of this type of lawn, but I should have thought that weeds must be a considerable problem. One can use a selective weed-killer on grass, but not on other sward-forming plants. Presumably, once the lawn is established, most of the weeds will be smothered, but it must require a great deal of attention in the early stages. Also, any alternative species must be able to withstand at least a certain amount of treading—this is surely the essential difference between a 'lawn' and 'ground cover'.

The most commonly used alternative species is Camomile, *Anthemis nobilis*, particularly its non-flowering cultivar 'Treneague', but this does not

concern us here because, like other constituents of 'alpine lawns', it needs an
open situation. Other species have been used—as early as 1859, species of
Sagina (pearlwort) were recommended for lawns. How widely this was used
I do not know, but in the Pacific north-west states of America, related species
are used as ground cover to some extent. *Sagina subulata* and *Minuartia verna*
(sometimes called *Arenaria verna*) and the golden-leaved variety 'Aurea' of
each are used on banks and in rock gardens. They are known as 'Scotch Moss'
and 'Irish Moss' (although they are not true mosses) and are sold in garden
shops as 4–6 inch (10–15 cm) squares, to be set about 6 inches (15 cm) apart
when they are planted. These grow in partial shade as well as full sun.

Dichondra repens is a creeping perennial that will grow in sun or shade. It
is able to withstand drought and is used for lawns in areas such as California
and the hotter parts of Europe, for example Italy. It has small round leaves
and nondescript flowers, and may be grown from either seed or offsets. It
stands treading quite well, and can tolerate a slight frost.

Helxine soleirolii, a native of the Balearics, Corsica and Sardinia, known
variously as Mind-your-own-business, Mother of Thousands and, most
appropriately, the Curse of Corsica, has been used to carpet banks, and cover
rocks in rock gardens. It grows best in shade—I have seen it covering the
rocks in a grotto where the light was very dim—and certainly makes an
effective mat over a vertical wall, but it is such a pernicious weed that I
hesitate to recommend anyone to introduce it deliberately, though some
people find it useful for its shade-tolerant qualities. I have seen it suggested
that this might be used as a lawn, but it does not take treading well and
needs stepping stones, and turns black with both drought and cold. It is not
very hardy and cannot stand heavy frost.

Real mosses of various kinds make a beautiful natural carpet in woodland
and it would be interesting to experiment with their use in areas of dense
shade. They are used quite extensively in Japanese gardens to cover the
ground between stones which are used as stepping stones—thus getting over
the problem of treading. The susceptibility of many species to drought
would be a problem in some areas.

Where ability to withstand treading is not necessary, but the visual
equivalent of a lawn is desired—that is, a smooth spread of green—there are
one or two possibilities. *Pachysandra terminalis*, Japanese Spurge, is widely
used for this purpose in the United States; it tolerates not only quite dense
shade, but dryness as well. Other shade-tolerant, low-growing evergreens
can be used in a similar way, for example ivy, and the greater and lesser
periwinkles, *Vinca major* and *V. minor*, particularly the latter, which makes a
denser cover. *Hypericum calycinum*, the Rose of Sharon, is slightly taller,
growing to about a foot (30 cm), but it is even more vigorous and can be

PLAN FOR WALLED COURTYARD

10 × 8 metres

Many of the plants will overhang the paving and soften the straight lines.

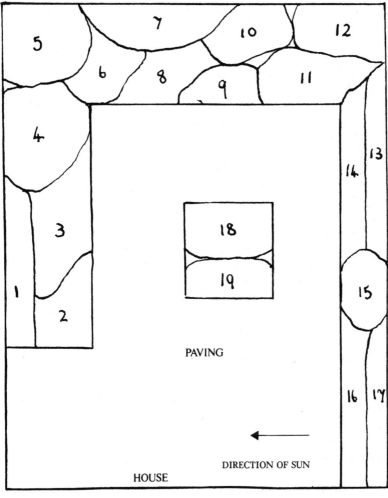

The exact species or variety is not given in many cases, where several members of a genus would be suitable.

1. Climbing rose, e.g. 'Mermaid'
2. Polyanthus
3. Hosta + *Narcissus bulbocodium*
4. *Mahonia japonica*
5. Pieris
6. Lilies
7. *Choisya ternata*
8. Dwarf rhododendron
9. Bergenia
10. Hydrangea
11. Ferns
12. Camellia
13. *Garrya elliptica*
14. Hellebores
15. *Fatsia japonica*
16. London Pride
17. *Jasminum nudiflorum*
18. Evergreen azaleas
19. Fuchsias

invasive. It is very useful, however, for clothing dry banks and has attractive yellow flowers like large buttercups. *H.* × *moseranum*, a cross between the last species and *H. patulum*, has arching reddish stems and can be used in a similar way.

Prostrate junipers are often planted for their spiky, horizontal shapes, particularly in rock gardens, but they can also be used *en masse*, when they form a sea-like expanse of dark green. They make a completely weed-suppressing ground cover, and grow well in shade, although preferably not under trees as dead leaves tend to catch in the branches and rot. These plants spread rapidly; planting 3–4 feet (around a metre) apart should give complete cover in 3–5 years' time, depending on how much moisture was available. Once established, junipers are able to stand a lot of drought. A number of varieties are suitable for use in this way, but in a shaded situation the best is *Juniperus* × *media* 'Pfitzerana'.

If there is no lawn, some sort of plain area or open space is still essential; this is easy to realise if one tries to visualise a garden that consists of simply one large flower-bed, or a continuous rock-garden. Paving, sand, pine-bark or gravel can be used for this place instead of grass or another type of plant. The first is the most practical and the majority of people find it the most attractive. It is probably the most expensive as regards original outlay, but if properly laid, no further expense is needed and little maintenance is required. The type of paving chosen depends on personal taste, depth of pocket, and the style and material of the house and any surrounding masonry. Stone slabs, attractive though they are, look somewhat out of place if surrounded by brick walls. Bricks themselves are sometimes used, also cobbles set in cement. These look well, particularly when used as a contrast in texture, but are difficult to walk on unless they are set in very flat. There are now many synthetic slabs available which are much cheaper, as a rule, than stone, and come in a variety of colours. I prefer neutral-coloured ones but this again is a matter of personal taste. A very small garden can be paved almost all over with spaces left round the edge for planting, and other plants grown in tubs. Sand, gravel and pebbles seem to be used extensively in Japanese gardens, often raked into patterns, but this style transplants uneasily to the western world.

To return to the plants in a garden, these can be thought of as occupying three layers—the trees, the shrubs and the ground layer. This can be seen in almost all natural woodlands. The first two layers are visible all year round in some form, whether as evergreens or a pattern of branches. They, therefore, provide the shape and framework of a garden and it is of vital importance that they should be carefully chosen.

The most important difference between trees and shrubs lies in habit rather than size. A tree has one main trunk (occasionally two or three) and in most cases is free from branches until a certain height above ground. Shrubs have many branches arising from ground level and so usually take up more space in a border than a tree. Many species of plant can be grown either as small trees or large shrubs. If a specimen is wanted as a tree, but seems to be growing naturally as a shrub, the strongest vertical shoot should be selected, staked if necessary, and subsidiary shoots cut out. Later, side branches can be trimmed to leave a clean stem to whatever height is desired. Occasionally, a specimen persists in putting out more shoots at ground level and has to be left as a bush, but usually this training is successful. Less often, the reverse is wanted—to turn a natural tree into a shrub. In this case, the trunk is cut back while the plant is young and usually a number of stems will develop— as in the coppicing of hazel.

A small garden should not have too many trees and these should be of suitable proportions. Trees that grow to a large size should never be planted near houses because, apart from the dense shade, their roots can impoverish soil and cause damage to buildings and drains. Ideally, trees in a garden should not provide too dense a shade, and the branches should start fairly high up the trunk (this of course can be adjusted by pruning). They should be deep-rooted—shallow roots are in competition for nutrients with other plants. Suitable shade trees for the average garden in cool or temperate climates include *Cornus florida*, *C. nuttallii* and *C. controversa*, small maples, cherries, crab-apples, magnolias and *Crataegus* species. Cherries and crabs are not suitable if the garden is already shaded, as they like an open position. In a large woodland garden, oaks form the ideal shade trees; they fulfil all the conditions mentioned and their leaves form a splendid leaf mould, of good texture and full of nutrients.

In a shaded garden, it is even more important than usual to consider the form and foliage of the plants used, as well as their flowers. This does not mean that one cannot have colour in a shaded garden, but it is not likely to produce the vivid display that a sunny one can. This need not be a drawback; after all:

'No white nor red was ever seen
So amorous as this lovely green.'

Most shrubs flower less freely in shade, but the flowers tend to last longer. Moreover, the effect and quality of colour are quite different in the shade from in the sun, just as sunlight of different intensities itself affects colour. Clothes that look bright and attractive in the Mediterranean or tropical sun look garish in paler, temperate lands and conversely, what seems a vivid colour in a cool climate looks pallid in the tropical sun.

Mauve, lilac and violet are colours that can look very washed-out and uninteresting in sunlight, but in shade—and at dusk—these colours often have a luminescence that seems to make them glow. This is noticeable in rhododendrons—*R. ponticum*, *R. rubiginosum* and even the spectacular *R. augustinii* are among those that appear a better, more intense colour in shade. White is always effective there, as are pale colours in general—pinks, apricots and lemons. Red, particularly a deep red such as crimson, tends to have a flat, two-dimensional look in shade, almost merging into the green background.

Any garden needs a backbone of evergreen shrubs, to give depth and interest all the year round. Too often, people seem to take 'evergreen' as being synonymous with conifer, and plant lots of cypresses in various shapes, colours and sizes. However, there are many good, flowering evergreens available, most of which, fortunately, prefer a shaded to a sunny position. These are given in detail in Chapter Five.

If possible, the foliage of these evergreens should vary in size, shape, colour and texture. This of course applies to deciduous plants as well, but it is more important for the evergreens, whose foliage provides interest throughout the year. Rhododendrons are especially valuable here as the species have particularly interesting foliage. Some have leaves of a beautiful glaucous blue-green—*R. campanulatum* var. *aeruginosum*, *R. oreotrephes*, *R. lepidostylum* and *R. thomsonii* come at once to mind. This is particularly useful as the grey- and silver-foliaged plants that are often used for contrast are all sun-lovers and cannot be used in a shady garden. The large-leaved rhododendrons are among the best foliage plants that can be grown in non-tropical gardens. They are very much woodland plants, and besides shade from too hot a sun, must have wind-shelter. *R. sinogrande* when young has dark, leathery leaves up to 3 feet (a metre) long. Once the plant is older and starts to flower, the leaves become slightly smaller. Other species with large leaves include *R. falconeri* (probably the hardiest and most easily grown of this group), *R. hodgsonii*, *R. macabeanum*, *R. arizelum* and *R. rex*. All of these are seen at their best in a climate where the humidity is usually high, such as the west coast of the British Isles, the Pacific coast of the United States and South Island, New Zealand, but they are also grown effectively in Australia, particularly around the Melbourne area, and in other parts of Britain. In drier areas, the leaves are smaller, but still impressive.

Another asset of many rhododendrons is a coloured indumentum. This is a coating of dense hairs on the underside of the leaves, usually reddish-brown in colour, which gives a beautiful effect when the leaves move in the wind. Species and hybrids with striking indumentum include *R. arboreum*, *R. fulvum*, *R. falconeri*, *R. bureavii* and 'Sir Charles Lemon'. Sometimes the whole of the young growth is covered with indumentum, often whitish at that

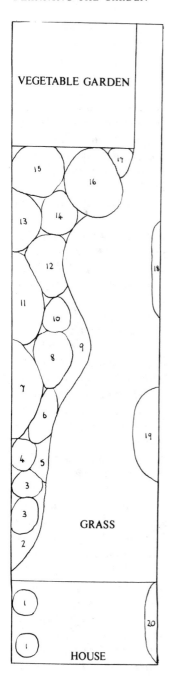

PLAN FOR LONG, NARROW GARDEN

20 × 5 metres

Surrounded by wall or high fence.

1. Camellias in tubs
2. *Ajuga reptans* 'Burgundy Glow' (or similar) + snowdrops
3. Evergreen azaleas
4. *Brunnera macrophylla*
5. Violets
6. Potentilla
7. Pieris
8. Rhododendron 'Elizabeth'
9. *Primula* species
10. Deciduous hybrid azalea or *Rhododendron atlanticum*
11. *Corylopsis* sp. underplanted with bluebells
12. *Hosta sieboldii* var. *elegans*
13. *Kerria japonica*
14. Lacecap hydrangea
15. *Viburnum rhytidophyllum* + *Geranium* species
16. *Acer palmatum dissectum*
17. *Meconopsis* species
18. Climbing rose 'Mermaid'
19. *Magnolia soulangeana* underplanted with *Cyclamen hederifolium*
20. Chaenomeles

DIRECTION OF SUN

stage, which later wears off the upper surface, as in *R. calophytum* and *R. yakushimanum*. Then again, the shapes of the leaves vary from being almost round, as in *R. orbiculare* and *R. williamsianum*, to narrow and pointed as in *R. makinoi* and *R. roxianum*. Fuller descriptions of these and other rhododendrons are given later.

Viburnum rhytidophyllum, the leatherleaf viburnum, has fairly large leaves with an interesting, bullate texture, reddish on the reverse, and is one of the best foliage plants for gardens that cannot grow rhododendrons because the soil is alkaline or the climate is not right. The large, lobed leaves of *Fatsia japonica* are interesting and seem particularly suited to town gardens. Bamboos provide a contrast in shape to almost anything else and always seem to have a slightly exotic air, though some species are rather invasive and are better planted in containers.

Except in hot climates, most ground-layer plants die back in winter, but the round, leathery leaves of the Bergenias persist throughout the year. Some turn bronze or reddish in winter. In summer, it is easy to have contrasts in foliage in the ground layer. Hostas have large, plain shapes and considerable variation in colour. *H. sieboldiana*, especially in the form 'Elegans', has beautifully textured blue-grey leaves, and there are many varieties with leaves variegated in different ways. Then there are the feathery leaves of *Dicentra spectabilis*, Dutchman's Breeks, and *Meconopsis cambrica*, the Welsh poppy. I recommend the latter with reservation—the bright green leaves and clear yellow flowers are delightful, but once you have it in a garden, you have it for life. It seeds itself freely, and unless unwanted seedlings are pulled up when very small, they are difficult to dislodge as they soon develop long tap roots. There is an orange colour that is much less desirable. There are a number of other species of *Meconopsis*, all shade-lovers, several of which have very decorative rosettes of leaves that persist for several years until the plant flowers. Some, however, are rather tricky, and they dislike too hot a climate.

Ferns are invaluable shade plants and they, too, provide variety in foliage effect—by no means all are 'ferny' in appearance. They were very popular in Victorian times and then suffered a long period of neglect, but there has been a welcome revival of interest in them in recent years. A hundred years ago or thereabouts, what must be the ultimate in shade gardens were designed for ferns—grottoes. These were virtually caves built into a hillside, or possibly in some cases the grotto came first and a hillock was constructed over it. They were built from large, rough pieces of rock, and there was usually a passage with a chamber at the end containing a pool and often a statue. A few panes of glass were set into the roof to allow a dim light to filter through, otherwise nothing would have grown and no one could have seen it anyway. Often, there was some arrangement of water pipes to let water trickle down inside and into the pool.

These were planted with ferns of various kinds and their relatives, Selaginellas. In one that I know, the Selaginella is being choked out by the invasive Helxine and the only ferns left are some plants of the male fern, *Dryopteris filix-mas*, and the hart's tongue, *Phyllitis scolopendrius*, which seems to have colonised every available crevice.

In the height of summer, a grotto must have been marvellously cool, and romantic and gothick too, but surely only to wander into and out again as even on the hottest day it must have been too dank and chill to sit there. I suppose no one will build grottoes again, but those that remain are well worth preserving as echoes of a past age.

Grottoes apart, the darkest gardens must be those of basement flats. Here, one can sometimes make use of artificial means to lighten the darkness. House walls are often colour-washed, but garden walls seldom are. Yet this can have a dramatic effect in lightening a small garden (or part of a larger one) particularly of the courtyard type. Usually in a garden of this kind, one wants to make as much use of space as possible, and grow climbing plants against every available wall. If these are tied to a trellis, which is then fixed to the wall, it is possible—just—to swing that away from the wall when it needs re-painting. Nothing looks dingier than a colour-washed wall once the colour starts to peel off and dirty strips appear.

3

Plants and their Environment

Before going on to deal with the various shade-tolerant plants in detail, it is worth discussing the tricky question of hardiness, and considering the various types of soil different plants need.

HARDINESS

Large countries like the United States and Australia obviously have considerable internal variations in climate and growing conditions. Even in small, compact countries like Britain, there are marked differences both between north and south, and east and west. The south of England has a growing season two or three weeks longer at each end of the summer than that of most of Scotland. The west coast of both England and Scotland is wetter and milder than the east. This suits many plants very well, for example rhododendrons, and leads to the strange situation of sub-tropical plants growing out-of-doors (at Inverewe Gardens in north-west Scotland) at a latitude similar to that of Labrador and further north than that of Moscow. This mildness is due to the warm currents of the Gulf Stream; a similar effect is noticeable on the Pacific north-west coast of the United States and Canada,

Desfontainea spinosa

where the Japan current has a moderating effect on the climate. The United States has been divided into 'hardiness zones' according to the degree of cold generally experienced in a particular area; these run horizontally across most of the continent and turn almost at right angles to run parallel to the west coast (any place on the west coast having much less severe winters than a place of the same latitude on the east coast). When a plant is described as being 'hardy to zone V', this means that it should be hardy in any place within zone V, and in zones with higher numbers. The lower the zone number, the lower the winter temperatures. The term 'hardiness' generally refers to winter cold, and this is the sense in which I have used it in this book, but in hot climates the term can sometimes be used to refer to heat resistance.

The climate in the British Isles is generally similar to that of the Pacific north-west coast of the USA, the southern part of British Columbia in Canada, and parts of South Island, New Zealand; but summers in these places tend to be warmer and drier, and there some shade at least is necessary for many plants that can be grown in full sun over much of Britain. Most plants which are mentioned later as being hardy only in milder areas of Britain and western North America would be expected to grow almost anywhere in Australia, given the correct cultural conditions.

Most of the British Isles is said to fall within the American hardiness zone VIII, with the coldest areas being equivalent to zone VII and the west coast to zone IX. There are, however, a number of anomalies. *Cornus capitata*, which is generally considered to be hardy only in the very mildest areas of Britain, is rated as VII–VIII in the States, the same as *Rhododendron falconeri*, which can be grown pretty well anywhere in Britain as long as it has sufficient moisture and shelter from wind. It is difficult, of course, to draw direct comparisons, because the hotter summers in the States ripen the wood more and so make a plant better able to withstand a cold winter.

While plants can be classified according to their cold-hardiness, it is inadvisable to be too dogmatic, as many species of plant have different forms, some of which may be hardier than others although they look very similar. It is well known among rhododendron growers that plants originating from material collected at a high altitude are frequently more cold-resistant than those descended from plants collected originally at a low altitude. The extent of snow cover in a plant's natural home is also important. It seems illogical that plants from high in the Himalayas are sometimes not hardy in much milder climates, but low-growing species such as dwarf rhododendrons and alpines are covered in winter by a blanket of snow which insulates them from the effects of severe frosts.

Other aspects of weather are also relevant. If the previous summer was sunny, and the wood is well-ripened, a plant is better able to withstand low

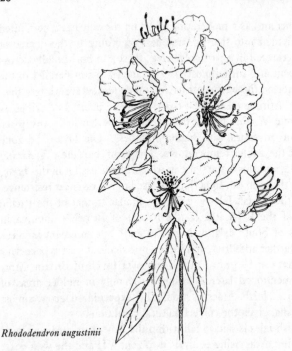

Rhododendron augustinii

temperatures. Also, the time at which a cold spell comes is important. Low temperatures in mid-winter, when plants are dormant, tend to do much less damage than a sudden cold spell either in early autumn while the wood is still soft, or in late spring after the new growth has started. Even plants which are basically very hardy can be damaged, if not killed, in this way. The beautiful pink deciduous azalea, *Rhododendron schlippenbachii*, is hardy to zone IV in the United States—which means it can withstand temperatures far lower than any likely to occur in Britain—but in England, the new growth starts at the end of March and, more often than not, is frosted, which means less growth later on and fewer flowers the following year.

There is not much one can do to counteract the effects of these late and early frosts. Continuing to water the garden too late into autumn tends to delay the ripening of wood, and should be avoided. It is probably safe to say that plants should not be watered after the end of the summer unless they actually seem to be on the point of dying from drought. If it is known that a district is liable to have these early or late frosts, it is better to avoid plants of doubtful hardiness. If very cold winters occur only rarely, it is reasonable to take a chance with slightly tender plants, but if severe winters occur as a matter of course, there is little point in trying them.

Even a single smallish garden can have several different microclimates.

Air drainage is of great importance when considering the effect of frost. Cold air is heavier than warm and so it tends to accumulate at the bottom of a slope. Gardens at the foot of a valley are often colder than those situated higher up on the slopes. Few gardens are completely level and it is worth placing plants at risk from frost, such as early rhododendrons, on the higher parts. With a sloping garden, a solid fence or wall at the lowest part acts as a barrier, and the cold air builds up against it, forming a frost pocket, whereas a light hedge or an open fence allows the cold air to move on and accumulate somewhere else.

It is well known that walls give protection to plants, and often varieties that are just too tender to be grown in the open in a particular area can be grown successfully against a wall, particularly a house wall. Even the best-insulated house will lose some heat to the outside through its walls—if you put your hand on a house wall on a cold day it will feel slightly warmer than, say, a wall at the end of the garden. One point to watch is that a plant at the foot of a wall is likely to dry out more quickly than one in the open garden, and it may possibly get little benefit from a light shower of rain. A wall also gives protection to plants with large leaves, such as *Fatsia japonica*, so that they are less liable to mechanical damage from wind.

Rhododendron moupinense

SOIL

Many plants are not fussy about the type of soil they grow in, but others are more particular. Some of the most beautiful shade-loving plants, including rhododendrons, pieris, enkianthus, camellias and most magnolias, will not grow in soil that contains chalk or lime. In these conditions, they are unable to take in adequate amounts of magnesium and iron, both essential elements, and become what is known as chlorotic, with leaves that are yellowish instead of a healthy green. If the soil is only marginally alkaline, it may be possible to modify it by digging in peat and leaf-mould from trees growing on acid soil, and adding iron sequestrene (although this is expensive). But if the soil is chalk or strongly alkaline, there is not much that can be done. The plants in

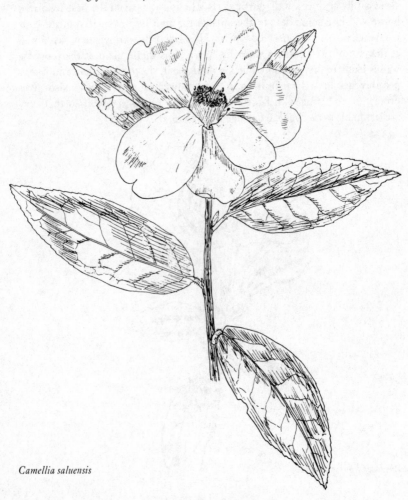

Camellia saluensis

question can be grown in tubs or a raised bed, but even then, there is likely to be a problem with watering unless there is an ample supply of rain-water, as the tap-water will usually be alkaline too. In these circumstances, it is best to forget about the lime-haters—there are other plants which can be used in their place.

Another reason for plants failing to grow well is poor drainage. Even species that need a great deal of water rarely like it standing around their roots for long periods. If a soil is waterlogged, the spaces between the particles are filled with water instead of air. Roots need oxygen to respire and grow, and so if they are standing in water for too long, the plant will die. Usually, quite a lot can be done to improve drainage. In a few cases, it may be necessary to lay pipes underground, but this is rare in gardens as houses are not often built on land as badly drained as this. If drainage is bad because the soil is heavy clay, which is the commonest reason, some sort of grit can be dug in. Probably the best is *weathered* boiler ash, if that can be obtained. If the ash is not well-weathered, it must be left standing in the garden for a month or two before use so that any harmful substances are washed out or broken down. Coarse sand or even fine gravel can be used.

Any sort of organic matter, such as peat, compost, leaf-mould or chopped straw, will also lighten heavy soil, but the effect will not be so long-lasting as all these are eventually broken down by soil bacteria. If fresh manure, newly fallen leaves or unrotted straw are used, it is necessary to add some nitrogenous fertiliser, as bacteria take nitrogen from the soil in the course of breaking it down. As already mentioned, these same organic materials can be used to improve the moisture-holding capability of a poor, dry soil.

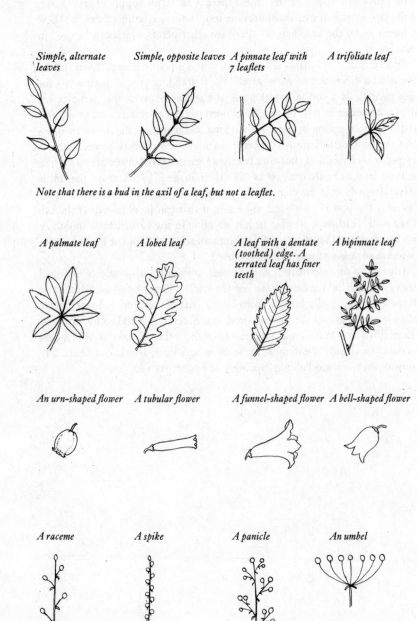

Simple, alternate leaves

Simple, opposite leaves

A pinnate leaf with 7 leaflets

A trifoliate leaf

Note that there is a bud in the axil of a leaf, but not a leaflet.

A palmate leaf

A lobed leaf

A leaf with a dentate (toothed) edge. A serrated leaf has finer teeth

A bipinnate leaf

An urn-shaped flower

A tubular flower

A funnel-shaped flower

A bell-shaped flower

A raceme

A spike

A panicle

An umbel

4

Trees

This chapter is confined to relatively small trees that will grow in woodland or in a sunless town garden. Large trees are shade-givers and, for the sake of space if nothing else, most be excluded.

I have tried to make this, and the following chapters on individual plants, as comprehensive as possible but I am sure there are omissions. I have not attempted to include native plants that are not commercially available, although there are many of these, particularly, perhaps, in Australia and New Zealand, that are well worth planting in gardens that can provide similar conditions to their natural habitats.

EVERGREENS

CORNUS

The Dogwoods or Cornels form a large and important genus, ranging from suckering shrubs to forest trees. Some are grown for their coloured stems; those that are planted for floral effect have 'flowers' of large bracts, with the real flowers in an inconspicuous cluster in the centre. Most are very hardy and easily grown. The shrubby species can be propagated by cuttings or layers and the trees from seed.

The diversity of the genus *Cornus* is such that it has now been split by botanists into several genera. *C. florida* and *C. nuttallii* are now called *Benthamidia*; *C. kousa* and *C. capitata* become *Benthamia*; the creeping dogwood and the dwarf cornel of the Highlands go into *Chamaepericlymenium*, and the wild dogwood of the chalk downs, along with the species *C. alba* and *C.*

stolonifera, are *Thelycrania*. Horti-culturalists, however, seem to be sticking to the old nomenclature—doubtless because of the unpronounceability of the new—and as it is under *Cornus* that the species mentioned here are likely to be found in catalogues and most reference books, I am using that name in this book.

C. capitata is unusual, both in being evergreen and in being slightly tender; it is hardy in Australia, New Zealand, western USA and the south-west of the British Isles. It does well in light woodland, where it can grow to 30 feet (9 metres) or more. It has yellow bracts 1½–2 inches (4–5 cm) long in summer, and large red fruits in autumn.

EMBOTHRIUM

E. coccineum is one of the most spectacular of all flowering trees. It has a tall, columnar habit and likes a

Embothrium coccineum

rapidly. 'Longifolium' has longer and narrower leaves, and is more evergreen but less hardy.

EUCRYPHIA

This is a beautiful genus of small trees, all with white flowers with a boss of golden stamens. All like a sheltered position on damp, lime-free soil with plenty of organic matter. They are southern hemisphere plants, from South America and Australasia, and are particularly useful in flowering in late summer.

moist, lime-free soil with plenty of humus and a sheltered situation. While it does particularly well in humid coastal areas, I have seen fine specimens in Surrey. There are a number of horticulturally distinct forms, but all are varieties of this one species. The typical variety comes from the southern tip of Chile and is fairly hardy; in favoured areas it can reach 40 feet (12 metres). It is more or less evergreen—some leaves are shed in a cold winter—and has odd, spiky, scarlet flowers in clusters along the branches in late spring/early summer. *E. coccineum* var. *lanceolatum* 'Norquinco Valley' was collected about 5,000 feet (1,500 metres) up in the Andes, and although it is the least evergreen form, it seems to be the hardiest—it will grow in the north of England if sheltered from east winds. It is certainly the most free-flowering; the clusters of flowers are so thick along the branches that they touch each other and the tree is a blaze of red. Once established—which may take some time—it grows

E. cordifolia is an upright tree that can reach 18–30 feet (5–9 metres), but is usually nearer the lower figure in cultivation. It comes from Chiloe, off the coast of Chile, and can stand some lime in the soil. It has heart-shaped leaves and white flowers 2½ inches (6 cm) across in late summer. It does well in Australia and New Zealand, but in the British Isles it is only hardy in the south and west.

E. lucida forms a tree about 20 feet (6 metres) high in Britain, but in its native Tasmania, I am told it can reach 60 feet (18 metres). The flowers are hanging and scented, and are early for the genus, opening in mid-summer.

E. × intermedia is a very fine hybrid between the last species and the deciduous *E. glutinosa*. The form most often available is called 'Rostrevor'. It is a fast-growing, upright small tree, with scented white flowers borne profusely in late summer/early autumn.

E. milliganii is a Tasmanian species that will tolerate some lime. It forms a small, columnar tree, sometimes a shrub, with very small leaves and cup-shaped flowers, freely borne. It is a most attractive plant.

E. × nymansensis (*E. cordifolia × E. lucida*) has flowers 3 inches (7·5 cm) in diameter in late summer/early autumn, produced freely after the tree has reached a certain age—it is slower to start than some of the others. One slight drawback is that the flowers often tend to be concentrated towards the top of the tree. It is one of the hardiest, but may lose most of its leaves in a cold winter. It forms a columnar tree up to 50 feet (15 metres) tall and will tolerate lime. 'Nymansay' is the form most often grown; 'Mount Usher' sometimes has double flowers.

MAGNOLIA

Magnolias need a rich soil, moist but well-drained; most dislike lime but they will grow on clay, and most are surprisingly tolerant of atmospheric pollution. The roots are fleshy and easily damaged, so transplanting is best done in spring, and it is even more important than usual that they are not allowed to dry out. Magnolias are very disease-free and do well in Australia, New Zealand and the United States. Most species are deciduous.

M. nitida is an attractive, compact species reaching about 25 feet (7·5 metres), but in Britain can only be grown in really mild areas such as Cornwall. It does well in Australia and New Zealand. The flowers are scented, about 3 inches (7·5 cm) across, white or pale yellow. It comes from China and Tibet and dislikes chalk and cold winds.

RHODODENDRON

This very large genus (almost a thousand species and even more hybrids) is one of the most useful of all, where it can be grown. No other group of plants has such a range of size—from large trees to prostrate mats—although the majority, I suppose, are medium-sized shrubs. They like a lime-free soil with plenty of humus, a good supply of water, but also good drainage. The large-leaved species, like all plants with big leaves, dislike wind and must have a sheltered position. Rhododendrons dislike hot sun and, in the south of England and most parts of North America, Australia and New Zealand where they are grown, should be given at least partial shade. In colder areas like Scotland and the north of England, more exposure can be given to encourage the formation of flower-buds. The tree species are essentially woodland plants. The hybrids, in general, are more tolerant of imperfect conditions (too much shade, too much sun, and too cold) than the species, but while their display of flower is usually lavish, their foliage tends to be much less varied and interesting.

The tree species with smaller leaves tend to be more easily grown than those with very large leaves.

R. campanulatum is a variable species, which can be a large bush or an almost columnar tree of about 20 feet (6 metres). The leaves are about 6 inches (15 cm) long, brown underneath, and the flowers vary from white to purple. 'Knaphill' is a good form with lavender-blue flowers. Var. *aeruginosum* has new growth of a startling blue-green.

R. falconeri can form a spreading tree to 40 feet (12 metres) or more, but is often considerably less. The trunk and branches are smooth reddish-brown; the leaves are dark and leathery above, thickly covered with a furry brown indumentum below and are usually about a foot (30 cm) long. The creamy flowers are in large, round trusses and open in late spring. It is an outstanding plant, and is probably the easiest and hardiest of the large-leaved species.

R. fictolacteum is a variable species, with leaves slightly smaller than those of the last species but again leathery and rusty brown below. It too is relatively hardy, and has cream flowers with a red blotch in late spring.

R. macabeanum is one of the best yellow rhododendrons, but unfortunately the flowers open in early spring, and so may be frosted. The leaves are usually about 1 foot (30 cm) long and 6 inches (15 cm) across, dark and leathery above, white and woolly below. The new growth is silvery.

R. rex also has big, leathery leaves, and can make a 40-foot (12-metre) tree. The flowers are white or pink, blotched with crimson, and open in late spring.

R. sinogrande has the most spectacular foliage in the genus, with leaves that can be as much as 3 feet (a metre) long and 1 foot (30 cm) across in young plants, silvery below and glossy above. The flowers open in spring, and are bell-shaped, cream with a red blotch, in huge trusses. This is definitely a woodland plant as the leaves need maximum shelter.

R. thomsonii makes an open tree, sometimes a large bush, up to 20 feet (6 metres) or so. It has smooth, peeling bark and oblong, blue-green leaves, not very large. The flowers are bell-shaped, waxy and blood-red, in loose trusses. A prospective buyer should stipulate that the plant must have red flowers, as there are a couple of forms with dingy flesh-pink flowers.

DECIDUOUS

ACER

There are over a hundred species of Maple, mostly deciduous. Most are grown for their attractive foliage and good autumn colour, and many have decorative bark. Many grow too large for the average garden, but there are quite a number of a suitable size.

They are useful both in light wood-land and in an ordinary, rather sunless garden. Maples are grown widely in the United States, Australia and Britain.

A. capillipes, from Japan, is one of the 'snake-bark' maples, with greenish bark striped with white, and pink young growth. The leaves turn orange and yellow in autumn.

A. circinatum, the Vine Maple, from North America, has almost round leaves that turn red and orange in autumn. It is hardy to zone V in the States, and is one of the few maples with attractive flowers; they are red and white and open in spring.

A. davidii is a Chinese species that can reach 30 feet (9 metres), but is usually less. It has green bark, streaked with white, and ovate leaves that turn to yellow and orange.

A. forrestii, also from China, is an elegant small tree with striped bark and red leaf-stalks and young stems. It does not grow on chalk.

A. ginnala is a tree of about 20 feet (6 metres) with whitish, scented flowers and three-lobed leaves that turn brilliant red in autumn, but quickly fall. It comes from Japan, and is extremely hardy— to zone II in the States.

A. griseum, the Paperbark Maple, is usually a small tree, although it can reach 40 feet (12 metres). The old bark peels off the trunk and main branches, revealing orange new bark underneath. The trifoliate leaves turn brilliant red and orange in autumn.

A. japonicum may be a small tree or a large shrub. The seven- to eleven-lobed leaves colour well in autumn. There are many forms, but all like a sheltered position, with damp but well-drained soil. Var. *aconitifolium* has deeply cut lobes; var. *aureum* has leaves that are pale yellow in spring and early summer, gradually darkening, and scorch in a hot sun.

A. palmatum, the Japanese Maple, is a shrub or small tree with five- to seven-lobed leaves. It likes a moist, rich soil, preferably without lime. It needs wind shelter as strong winds shrivel up the new growth, but it is very hardy—zone V in the States. There are many cultivars, only a few of which can be mentioned here. 'Atropurpureum' is a beautiful tree with bronze-red leaves that turn deeper red in autumn. It is slow-growing, and not always easy to establish—I think good drainage is important. 'Aureum' has yellow leaves. 'Dissectum' has deeply-cut leaves and forms a dense, mounded shrub rather than a tree. There are also forms called 'Dissectum Aureum' and 'Dissectum Atropurpureum' with yellow and purple leaves respectively, 'Dissectum Palmatifidum' with leaves more finely divided and 'Dissectum Variegatum', which has bronze-red leaves, some tipped with cream or pink. 'Heptalobum' has larger, seven-lobed leaves and again this comes in different colour forms including 'Lutescens' (yellow) and 'Purpureum' (purple). 'Heptalobum Osakasuki', sometimes just called 'Osakasuki', has probably the most brilliant autumn colour of all the Japanese maples. 'Senkaki', the Coral Bark Maple, has coral red young branches, which look very effective in winter. It is more upright in growth than most forms of *A. palmatum* and can reach 30 feet (9 metres).

A. pensylvanicum, the Moosewood, has green young stems streaked with white and three-lobed leaves that turn yellow in autumn. It comes from eastern North America, and prefers a chalk-free soil.

CORNUS
See also p. 25.

C. controversa is a tree that can reach 30 feet (9 metres), occasionally more, whose branches grow in horizontal layers so that it reminds one of an outsize cake-stand. It has creamy flowers in late spring/early summer that have a lacy effect, followed by black fruit. The leaves turn reddish-purple in autumn. It is a most striking species that is surprisingly seldom seen. It is native to Japan and China. 'Variegata' has white-variegated leaves.

C. florida, the Flowering Dogwood, from the eastern United States, makes a small tree or sometimes a large shrub up to 20 feet (6 metres) tall. Four large white bracts surround the flowers in late spring/early

summer. It is a lovely tree, but dislikes chalk. The leaves turn red and purple in autumn. 'Rubra' has rose-pink bracts and reddish foliage; 'Tricolor' has leaves edged with white and tinged with pink. 'White Cloud' is a very free-flowering clone, with pure white bracts and bronze foliage.

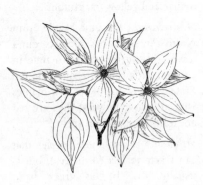

Cornus kousa

C. kousa is another species with a tiered growth habit, although not usually quite as marked as that of *C. controversa*. It is a small tree or large shrub, to about 20 feet (6 metres), that is smothered in white 'flowers' in summer, followed by red, strawberry-like fruits. It comes from Japan and Korea. Var. *chinensis*, the Chinese form, is slightly taller and more open-growing with larger bracts, and is more lime-tolerant than the typical form.

C. nuttallii, from the west of the USA, is a handsome tree that usually grows to about 25 feet (7·5 metres) in cultivation, although it can reach 80 feet (24 metres) in the wild. Its large white bracts, sometimes tinged with pink, give the effect of flowers 4–5 inches (10–12 cm) across. It is a startling display and lasts for some weeks, usually throughout late spring/early summer. It is reputed to like its roots shaded, but its head in the sun; again, it dislikes chalk. 'Gold Spot' is a form with leaves mottled with yellow.

Enkianthus campanulatus

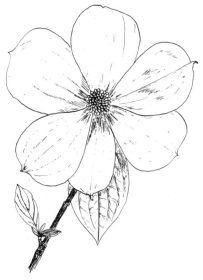

Cornus nuttallii

ENKIANTHUS

An attractive genus of small trees and shrubs that like a moist, humus-rich, lime-free soil with light shade. They should do well both in woodland and in a town garden if the right soil conditions can be given.

E. campanulatus has hanging racemes of bell-shaped, creamy flowers, usually veined with red, in late spring/

early summer. It has neat, dark leaves, usually turning red and yellow in autumn. It grows 10–15 feet (3–4 metres) tall and comes from Japan.

E. chinensis is taller, reaching about 20 feet (6 metres), with hanging clusters of yellow, bell-shaped flowers veined with red. Again, it has good autumn colour. It comes from China and Upper Burma.

EUCRYPHIA
See also p. 26.

E. glutinosa is probably the hardiest of the genus, to zone VII-VIII in the States, and is one of the finest of all flowering trees. The white flowers with their boss of red-gold stamens are 2–3 inches (5–7 cm) across and open in late summer. It has glossy, pinnate leaves that turn orange-red in autumn. It needs a rich, damp soil and, given these conditions, grows quickly and flowers when quite young. It comes from Chile.

Eucryphia glutinosa

Halesia monticola

HALESIA

These are small trees with white, bell-shaped flowers in late spring/ early summer, followed by winged fruit. They are hardy (zone IV–V in the USA), but like a deep, moist soil and a sheltered position. They do well in Australia.

H. carolina, the Snowdrop tree, can reach 30 feet (9 metres), and is very attractive when covered with its hanging, snowdrop-like flowers before the leaves open. It comes from the south-east United States.

H. diptera is similar, but only reaches about 10 feet (3 metres) and is sometimes shrubby. It has slightly larger flowers less freely produced.

H. monticola can reach 100 feet (30 metres) in the wild, but rarely exceeds 30 feet (9 metres) in cultivation. It has the typical snowdrop flowers, larger than the others. 'Rosea' has pale pink flowers, and var. *vestita* has flowers about 1½ inches (4 cm) long, sometimes

tinged with pink. This species also comes from the southern USA.

MAGNOLIA
See also p. 27.

M. denudata, the Yulan, is a small tree (occasionally a large shrub) growing to 25–30 feet (7–9 metres) with scented, white, waxy flowers in spring. It dislikes chalk, but is tolerant of atmospheric pollution. It is a native of China.

M. hypoleuca, still often known by its old name *M. obovata*, is a fair-sized tree with scented, creamy-white flowers with red stamens, up to 8 inches (20 cm) across, in summer. The bright red fruits that follow are also striking. It comes from Japan and dislikes lime.

M. kobus is a very hardy small tree from Japan that grows on any soil. It produces white flowers in spring before the leaves, but not until it is 12–15 years old. Some forms are never very free-flowering.

'Kewensis' is a hybrid between the

last species and *M. salicifolia*. It has 2 inch (5 cm) white flowers opening in spring before the leaves.

M.×loebneri (*M. kobus*×*M. stellata*) is a free-flowering small tree or large shrub, with narrow-petalled white flowers open in spring before the leaves. It does well on chalk. 'Leonard Messel' is a beautiful clone with pink flowers.

M. salicifolia is one of the species I like best, and is very suitable for the average garden. It is hardy and easily grown, forming a small tree with narrow, willowy leaves and scented white flowers in spring, before the leaves appear. If you scrape a bit of bark, it smells of lemon. It flowers young, usually at 5–6 years old, and is native to Japan. 'Jermyns' is a clone with larger flowers and broader leaves.

M. sieboldii is a small tree or a spreading shrub with scented, white cup-shaped flowers with crimson stamens produced off and on throughout the summer. It comes from Japan.

Magnolia sieboldii

M. sinensis has pendant white flowers, 5 or 6 inches (12–15 cm) across, with red stamens, in summer. It comes from west China and will grow on chalk. It forms a spreading tree or a large shrub.

Magnolia sinensis

M. wilsonii is very similar—almost identical in flower—but the leaves are narrower, and it usually has a more erect habit. It is probably the hardiest of the Chinese magnolias, if given adequate shade.

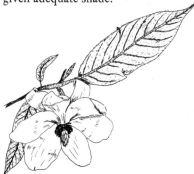

Magnolia wilsonii

STEWARTIA

This genus is related to Camellia, and also likes a shaded situation and moist, lime-free, humus-rich soil. Stewartias are beautiful in flower, although the display is not long-lasting, and most also have good autumn colour and attractive bark.

S. koreana, from Korea, is a small- to medium-sized tree with wide-open white flowers in late summer, beautiful peeling bark and vivid orange-scarlet autumn colour.

S. malacodendron is a small tree or large shrub, with solitary flowers about 3 inches (7·5 cm) across, white with purple stamens, in mid- to late summer. It comes from the southern USA, and in that country is given a hardiness rating of VII.

S. pseudocamellia, from Japan, is hardier (zone V) and makes a small tree with peeling bark and pointed leaves that colour well in autumn. The flowers are cup-shaped, white with yellow stamens, in mid- to late summer. This is the species most often grown.

STYRAX

Beautiful trees and shrubs requiring a lime-free soil, with hanging, white, bell-shaped flowers. Some species are rather tender. They are popular in the milder parts of the USA, and in Australia are most successful in the Dadenong ranges near Melbourne. They grow well in woodland conditions. There are a number of fairly similar species; I am only mentioning two of the hardiest ones (zone V in the States).

S. japonica is the most often grown species. It is an elegant, spreading tree, sometimes a large shrub, with oblong leaves. The white flowers hang in profusion from the undersides of the branches in summer. It comes from Japan and Korea. Var. *fargesii* is a Chinese form that is larger, with bigger leaves.

S. obassia, also from Japan, is a small, open tree with hanging racemes of white, bell-shaped flowers in summer. The leaves are roundish and furry below.

Stewartia pseudocamellia

5

Evergreen Shrubs

ABELIA

A. × *grandiflora* (*A. chinensis* × *A. uniflora*) is a member of a sun-loving genus which is included here because, although it probably does better in sun, it also grows and flowers well even in quite heavily shaded positions. It is what is usually called semi-evergreen, that is, the colder the winter, the more leaves it loses. It is hardy in all but the coldest areas of Britain, and in the western United States. It grows to about 5 feet (1·5 metres) and has tubular, pink-tinged white scented flowers borne profusely over a very long period—through the summer until autumn.

ARCTERICA

A. nana is the only species in this genus. It belongs to the Ericaceae, the heath family, and as with so many of these dislikes lime and likes good drainage. It comes from Japan and Kamchatka and grows only a few inches high, with scented, white, urn-shaped flowers in late spring.

ARCTOSTAPHYLOS

Another ericaceous genus, this time containing quite a number of species, many from the Pacific coast of the United States. In general, they are sun-lovers, but at least two of the dwarf species will also form a ground cover in shade. All require an acid soil.

A. nevadensis is a prostrate species from California with white, urn-shaped flowers followed by red fruit.

A. uva-ursi, Bearberry, is found wild both in Britain and the United States. It, too, is prostrate and spreading, with pale pink, urn-shaped flowers in spring, and red fruit.

ARDISIA

A. japonica, from Japan, is a dwarf evergreen with glossy leaves 4–5 inches (10–12 cm) long and pale pink flowers in spring followed by showy red berries. It is hardy on the Pacific coast of America and in mild areas of Britain. It is an attractive plant that is not well known; it must have a lime-free soil and quite a deeply shaded position.

AUCUBA

A. japonica, known variously as Japanese Laurel, Spotted Laurel and Gold-dust plant, is a large shrub that will grow even in dense shade. It was popular in Victorian shrubberies and became rather despised as a result, but is now looked on with more favour again. The typical form has large, pointed leaves, but it is most often seen in one of its variegated forms. It is widely grown in Australia, where shade is quite essential, and in the milder areas of America. It is hardy pretty well anywhere in Britain. It is dioecious, that is, male and female flowers are borne on different plants, and as the female develops attractive red berries, it is worth planting both sexes if it is grown at all. 'Gold Dust' is a female form with leaves blotched with gold, and 'Variegata' has smaller gold markings. Of the male forms, 'Crotonifolia', with conspicuous gold blotches, and 'Speckles' are probably the best. It is a large shrub when fully grown, 10–12 feet (2–4 metres) high and as much across, but few plants thrive with as little sun, and it also grows in dry situations.

AZARA

These are small evergreen trees or shrubs, all from Chile. All are rather similar, with yellow stamens forming the showy part of the flower and giving a mimosa-like effect. Most are tender, and are often grown with wall protection in Britain.

A. integrifolia is a tall-growing shrub with glossy oval leaves, flowering in early spring. 'Variegata' has leaves marked with pink and cream.

A. lanceolata is reasonably hardy; it grows in light woodland at Wisley in Surrey, and has been grown successfully against a south wall in Edin-

burgh (where it obviously requires sun rather than shade). It can reach 20 feet (6 metres) in height and has lots of small, scented, mustard-coloured flowers in late spring. The young leaves are covered with a brownish down.

Azara lanceolata

A. microphylla is probably the hardiest specimen. It has ascending branches which give it a narrow habit and it grows from 12 to 20 feet (4–6 metres) tall. The small, scented flowers open from early to mid-spring. 'Variegata' has leaves edged with yellow.

Azara serrata

A. serrata is still sometimes known by its old name, *A. dentata*. It is a tall shrub with scented, pale yellow flowers in early spring, and leathery, toothed leaves. Hillier's say it has withstood 15⁰C of frost without damage, but it is usually recommended for mild areas. I have not grown it myself and so have no personal experience.

BERBERIS

This is a large genus (about 450 species) that includes a number of useful garden species and hybrids. The flowers are yellow or orange and there is often an autumn display of fruit, or foliage in the case of the deciduous kinds. Most are easily grown, on any soil and in sun or shade. There is room here to mention only a few.

B. darwinii is one of the showiest, with dense clusters of orange flowers in spring (occasionally more in autumn) and small, dark, glossy leaves, three-spined at the tip. It comes from Chile and Argentina and forms a dense bush up to 10 feet (3 metres) tall. It is hardy to zone VII in the States. It is better with shelter from cold winds.

B. hypokerina is smaller, with leaves about 4 inches (10 cm) long, silvery below. It has purple stems and dark blue berries. It was introduced from Upper Burma by Kingdon Ward, who called it Silver Holly.

B. linearifolia has deep orange-red flowers, probably the richest colour in the genus, and narrow, dark glossy leaves. It grows about 4 feet (1·2 metres) tall and comes from Chile. 'Orange King' has larger, orange flowers.

Berberis linearifolia

Berberis darwinii

B. × lologensis is a natural hybrid between the last species and *B. darwinii*, found in Argentina. It has yellow flowers and glossy leaves.

B. × *stenophylla* is a graceful shrub about 8 feet (2·4 metres) tall, with arching branches and masses of yellow flowers in spring. There are many named clones, including 'Autumnalis', which has a second crop of flowers in autumn; 'Coccinea', which is smaller and has red buds opening to orange; and 'Pink Pearl', with flowers varying from red to orange, pink or bicoloured on the same plant and leaves that may be green or striped with pink and cream.

B. valdiviana is a largish species from Chile with big, leathery, almost spineless leaves, coppery when young, and masses of yellow flowers.

BUXUS

The boxes are usually grown as hedges or as clipped specimen bushes. The flowers are insignificant, but they grow on any soil, including virtually pure chalk, and in sun or dense shade.

B. sempervirens, Common Box, is almost too well known to need description. It stands clipping very well and its small, glossy leaves are neat and attractive, but if left to its own devices it will grow into a small tree. There are a great many cultivars, including several variegated forms. 'Argentea' has white-bordered leaves; 'Aureovariegata' has leaves marked with pale yellow. 'Gold Tip' is one of the most frequently planted cultivars—some of the leaves near the top of the shoots have yellow tips. 'Suffruticosa' is the dwarf form that is often used to edge beds and paths in a formal garden.

B. microphylla is a smaller growing species with a compact habit of growth.

CAMELLIA

For many years, camellias were treated as conservatory plants, but in fact most are very hardy. Along with rhododendrons, they form the most important group of plants for the shaded garden—the lime-free one, that is. They like very much the same conditions as rhododendrons—a moist, peaty, acid soil—but are as a rule more tolerant of traces of lime and of exposure to sun. There are about seventy species, but relatively few are widely grown. Most garden camellias are cultivars of *C. japonica*, a native of Japan and Korea which has long been grown in gardens in the Far East. Today, they are widely grown in the USA, Australia, the British Isles and New Zealand—many of the best modern hybrids come from New Zealand. Most flower from mid- to late spring.

I can only mention a few of the many cultivars available.

'Adolphe Audusson'—red, semi-double, with conspicuous gold stamens.

'Alba Plena'—large, double white.

'Apollo'— deep rose-red, sometimes with white blotches, semi-double. A good garden plant.

Camellia japonica 'Arejishi'

'Arejishi'—deep red-pink, paeony form, markedly toothed leaves.

'Berenice Boddy'—semi-double light pink.

'Contessa Lavinia Maggi'—large, double white or pale pink, striped with deeper pink.

'Donckelarii'—semi-double red, often marked with white. A good garden plant.

'Drama Girl'—semi-double, deep salmon pink, vigorous.

'Elegans'—deep peach pink; large, anemone form.

'Gloire de Nantes'—large, semi-double deep pink; compact.

'Guilio Nuccio'—very large, semi-double deep pink.

'Haku-rakuten' — white, semi-double.

'Jupiter'—bright red, single or semi-double, showy golden stamens; a very fine garden plant.

'Lady Clare'—deep pink, large and semi-double with spreading habit.

'Lady de Saumarez'—red blotched with white, semi-double, with compact growth. A sport of 'Tricolor'.

'Lady Vansittart' — white striped pink, semi-double.

'Magnoliiflora'—pale pink, double or semi-double, very distinctive with pointed petals in a beautiful regular arrangement.

'Mathotiana' — large, crimson, double.

'Mercury' — soft crimson, semi-double with a flatter flower than 'Jupiter'; compact growth.

'Nobilissima'—white, double, very early-flowering.

'Tricolor'— white streaked red, semi-double, compact.

Camellias are very long-lived—I have seen several plants reputed to be over a hundred years old, and they were vigorous and flowering freely. They make good tub plants, both these *japonicas* and the *williamsii* hybrids, although when they are in flower they may require a bucket of water a day. Varieties with a compact growth habit are best for this purpose. The whites, although they can be very beautiful, are rather unsatisfactory for the open garden in an area of high rainfall, as the petals are turned brown by rain, and look best under glass.

C. cuspidata is a large shrub, with pointed glossy leaves, bronze when young, and small, white flowers.

'Cornish Snow', a cross between this species and *C. saluensis*, is a charming and elegant plant, fairly large and

Camellia 'Cornish Snow'

loose-growing, with masses of small white flowers along the branches and very glossy, pointed leaves. 'Michael' is a clone with larger flowers, and 'Winton' is pale pink.

C. reticulata forms a large bush; the typical variety is fairly hardy, but the named clones are much less so. The wild type has large, single pink flowers, produced from late winter to spring, and leathery leaves with a conspicuous network of veins. It was discovered by George Forrest in west China in 1924, although cultivated forms had been known in the west since Robert Fortune sent home the semi-double 'Captain Rawes' in 1820.

'Buddha' is strong-growing, and has very large, pink, semi-double flowers with wavy petals.

'Captain Rawes' is deep rose-red, semi-double and very large.

'Lion Head'—deep red, very large, double.

'Mary Williams—large, single, crimson.

'Noble Pearl'—very large, semi-double red flowers.

'Purple Gown'—red-purple, striped with white, double flowers up to 8 inches (20 cm) across.

'Trewithen Pink'—large, pink, semi-double; hardier than the other named clones.

Many of these have been grown in China for probably several centuries. They do very well in Australia, New Zealand and the southern states of America.

'Inspiration' is a hybrid of *C. reticulata* with *C. saluensis*. It is semi-double, with bright pink flowers and neat, upright growth.

'Leonard Messel' (*C. reticulata* × *C. × williamsii* 'Mary Christian') is rich pink with prominent gold stamens, semi-double, hardy and free-flowering.

C. saluensis has very glossy, pointed leaves and single pink flowers, freely borne, in spring. It comes from western China.

'Salutation' (*C. saluensis* × *reticulata*) has silvery pink flowers, semi-double and 5 inches (12·5 cm) across, from late winter to spring.

C. sasanqua does not like a lot of shade in a temperate climate, but is good in shade in a sub-tropical one. It is less hardy than *C. japonica*. It has smallish, scented white flowers in winter and early spring. Again, there are many varieties:

'Brier Rose'—single pink flowers.

'Hiryu'—double red.

'Narumi-gata'—large white flowers, tinged with pink.

'Tricolor'—white, striped red and pink, single.

'Variegata'—white flowers tinged with pink, and grey-green leaves with a white edge.

C. × *williamsii* (*japonica* × *saluensis*). These plants are among the most valuable that can be grown in any lime-free garden. They flower profusely over a long period, from mid-winter in some cases to late spring/early summer, and I have even seen flowers encrusted with frost and remain undamaged. They are vigorous growers and are more satisfactory than the *japonica*s in climates like that of Scotland. Most of the cultivars are pink, but recently some good reds have been bred, many in New Zealand, and more varieties are coming onto the market all the time.

'Anticipation'—double, rosy crimson, very large. The richest colour I have yet seen in a *williamsii* camellia.

'Charles Colbert'—an Australian hybrid distinguished by its narrow, upright growth habit. Semi-double, creamy pink flowers.

'Charles Michael'—pale pink, single flowers.

'Citation'—large, silvery pink, semi-double, strong growing.

'Debbie'—a New Zealand hybrid

with rose-pink, paeony flowers over a long period. Vigorous and upright.

'Donation'—clear pink flowers with darker veining, semi-double, very free-flowering in late spring. Probably the only fault is that the side branches are sometimes bent right down with the weight of flowers. If there is room for only one camellia, this is the one to choose.

Camellia × *williamsii* 'Donation'

'Elsie Jury'—very large, clear pink flowers.

'Francis Hanger'—single white, prominent gold stamens, very elegant.

Camellia × *williamsii* 'Francis Hanger'

'J. C. Williams'—single pink, gold stamens.

'Mary Christian'—smallish, single pink flowers that do not open fully.

Camellia × williamsii 'Mary Christian'

CEPHALOTAXUS

These are coniferous trees, similar to and related to Yews, but with larger leaves. They prefer shade, even dense shade, and grow on chalk.

C. fortunei, Chinese Plum Yew, is a large, spreading shrub, occasionally a small tree, with dark glossy leaves up to 2 inches (5 cm) long. 'Prostrata' is a low-growing, prostrate form that makes a good ground cover.

C. harringtonia drupacea, Japanese Plum Yew, is similar to the last species, but has usually a denser habit of growth.

CHAMAEDAPHNE

C. calyculata 'Leatherleaf' is the only species in the genus which belongs to the family Ericaceae and like so many others of that family, dislikes lime. It is small growing with arching branches and white flowers in early spring.

CHOISYA

C. ternata, the Mexican Orange, has glossy, glandular, trifoliate leaves and white, scented flowers in early summer. It will reach 6 feet (2 metres) or more, but can be cut back after flowering if it gets too big. It is one of those adaptable plants that will grow in full sun or quite dense shade, and on any soil, although the leaves tend to turn yellowish if it is given too much water. The wood is brittle and can break under a heavy load of snow, so the branches should be shaken clear if possible.

Choisya ternata

CLEYERA

Evergreen trees and shrubs in the same family as *Camellia* and, like that, intolerant of lime.

C. fortunei has glossy leaves up to 6 inches (15 cm) long, bordered with white and marked with grey and pink. The young growth is reddish. The waxy, white, bell-shaped flowers are produced in late summer and autumn. It is slightly tender, but grows as far north as Edinburgh in a sheltered site. It has recently been introduced to Australia, where it is hardy and seems to be doing well. It comes from Japan.

C. japonica has waxy, white, scented flowers hanging from the undersides of the branches in late summer and dark, glossy leaves. It can grow quite large. It is one of those plants that make no great impact at a distance, but is pleasant and interesting at close range.

Cleyera japonica

COTONEASTER

A large genus, varying in size from prostrate shrubs to small trees, that are grown mainly for their bright red berries, but are also attractive in flower. Most are deciduous and a selection of these will be mentioned in the next chapter. They grow on any soil and in sun or shade.

C. buxifolius is dwarf in habit, with small leaves and red berries.

C. congestus is a creeping species that forms dense mounds.

C. dammeri is a prostrate species that will cover a bank with its long, trailing shoots. It will grow under other shrubs.

C. microphyllus is a small-leafed species often used for covering a low wall. Var. *thymifolius* has even smaller leaves.

CRINODENDRON

A Chilean genus, still sometimes known by its old name of *Tricuspidaria*. They like a lime-free, humus-rich soil and partial shade; although they are not suitable for cold areas they dislike dry heat and exposure to a lot of sun. They do well in Australia and New Zealand, given the right conditions. In Britain, they thrive on the west coast as far north as Inverewe in Wester Ross, and in Ireland, and can be grown in southern England.

C. hookeranum, sometimes called the Lantern Tree, is a plant that always

Crinodendron hookeranum

a shrub growing to 4–6 feet (1–2 metres) that has both deciduous and evergreen forms, the latter being taller and less hardy. It has racemes of white flowers from mid- to late summer, and the leaves turn red in autumn.

DANAE

D. racemosa is not showy but is attractive nonetheless, with neat, glossy leaves on arching branches. It is small-growing, with inconspicuous flowers that are sometimes followed by red berries.

DAPHNE

A genus of beautiful, scented plants which should be planted near a path where they can be seen at close range and their fragrance appreciated. It is the calyx that is coloured and not the petals. They are widely grown in Australia and New Zealand.

causes comment when it is well grown. It has dark, glossy leaves and fleshy crimson flowers hanging on long stalks in summer. It forms a large shrub, up to 20 feet (6 metres) or more, or even a large tree.

C. patagua is less showy, with white, bell-shaped flowers in late summer. It grows to 20 or 30 feet (6–9 metres) in cultivation, but can reach 70 feet (21 metres) in the wild.

CYRILLA

C. racemiflora 'Leatherwood' is the only species. It is native to the southeast USA, Central America and the northern part of South America. It is

Daphne blagayana

D. blagayana is low-growing with long, trailing branches with spurge-like, grey-green leaves at their ends. These long shoots should be pegged down and covered with soil so that they can root as they go along. The flowers are strongly scented, creamy white, in clusters from early to mid-spring. It likes a lime-free soil with plenty of humus, but is not always easy to satisfy. It has whitish berries, but my plant has never produced any. It comes from the mountains of S. E. Europe, and does not like too dense a shade.

D. laureola, Spurge Laurel, is a British native that will grow in really dense shade, on moist soils, though it does best in alkaline conditions as long as it is not too dry. It can grow up to about 4 feet (1·2 metres) tall and has greenish-yellow scented flowers in early spring.

D. odora is a native of China and Japan that grows to about 4 feet (1·2 metres) with a similar spread.

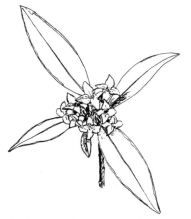

Daphne odora 'Aureomarginata'

The scented pink flowers open in early spring. The typical form with dark green leaves is slightly tender, but 'Aureomarginata', which has leaves bordered with white, is both hardier and more vigorous. It grows in sun or in shade, preferably not too dense.

D. pontica is a woodland plant that likes a humus-rich soil. Like *D. laureola*, it is not showy, again with yellow-green flowers from mid- to late spring, but is also useful for its tolerance of low light intensity.

DESFONTAINEA

D. spinosa is a lovely shrub from Chile and Peru that needs a moist, lime-free, humus-rich soil and a shaded site—similar conditions to *Crinodendron hookeranum*. It is successful in favourable areas in Australia and New Zealand, and in Britain does particularly well along the west coast. It forms a dense bush 8–10 feet (2–3 metres) tall, with spiny, holly-like leaves and tubular scarlet flowers, yellow at the mouth, from mid-summer on until autumn. 'Harold Comber' is a form with larger, more vivid red flowers.

DRIMYS

A genus of evergreen shrubs or small trees from the southern hemisphere, related to the Magnoliaceae.

D. lanceolata (still sometimes referred to by its old name of *D. aromatica*) grows to about 12 feet

(3·6 metres) and has handsome, red-stemmed, aromatic leaves, bronze when young, and inconspicuous white flowers in late spring. It is native to S. E. Australia. It and the next species do best in a sheltered situation, such as light woodland; although it is generally considered rather tender, it is recorded as growing in Edinburgh.

D. winteri, Winterbark, is an elegant large shrub from S. America, sometimes a small tree, with large, leathery leaves and scented umbels of white flowers in late spring/early summer. Var. *andina* is a dwarf form.

EPIGAEA

Dwarf, creeping evergreens belonging to the Ericaceae that like a moist, lime-free soil with plenty of humus. They are naturally woodland plants.

E. asiatica is a Japanese species with pink, urn-shaped flowers in spring.

E. gaultherioides, once known as *Orphanidesia gaultherioides*, is a pretty, trailing plant with large, saucer-shaped flowers and hairy leaves. It comes from the Black Sea area and dislikes exposure to sun and wind.

E. repens, the Mayflower or Trailing Arbutus, has heads of scented pink and white flowers in late spring. It comes from eastern North America.

FATSIA

F. japonica is a shrub that always seems particularly suited to town gardens. It has rather an exotic appearance, with large, palmate, glossy leaves, and is one of those plants of considerable architectural value. It has panicles of white flowers in autumn. It looks as if it should be tender, but is reasonably hardy (to zone VII in the States). It is tolerant of atmospheric pollution and grows in light or deep shade. It does well in Australia as long as sufficient shade is provided.

× FATSHEDERA (FATSIA × HEDERA)

× *F. lizei* is a fine example of that rather unusual thing, a bigeneric hybrid. It likes similar conditions to the last species, one of its parents, and is not dissimilar in appearance although the leaves are smaller and the growth habit is taller and laxer.

GAULTHERIA

A large, ericaceous genus that likes moist, lime-free soil and a shaded position. Many will grow in dense shade and as most are low-growing and spreading, they make useful ground cover in such situations. They are widely grown in the Pacific states of America, where several are natives.

G. adenothrix is a dwarf Japanese species with neat leathery leaves and urn-shaped pinkish white flowers in summer, followed by red fruits.

G. humifusa grows barely 4 inches (10 cm) tall with leaves about ½ inch

(1 cm) long. It too has pink-white flowers followed by red berries. It comes from N. W. America.

G. ovatifolia comes from the same area and is similar but slightly taller—to about a foot (30 cm)—with bigger leaves.

G. procumbens, Wintergreen or Partridge Berry, comes from the eastern United States and Canada and is extremely hardy. It grows about 6 inches (15 cm) high and makes an excellent ground cover, with dark green leaves and red berries in autumn.

G. shallon, Salal, is another native of western America. It is a vigorous species, growing 4 or 5 feet (up to 1·5 metres) high or even more in a moist situation. It has dark green, leathery, rounded leaves and pale pink, urn-shaped flowers followed by edible purple berries. It is very

Gaultheria shallon

vigorous and spreading and has become naturalised in some places in Britain as it has been widely planted as a cover for pheasants.

G. trichophylla is a dwarf Japanese species with pink flowers followed by large, bright blue berries. It is not as hardy as the American species.

GAYLUSSACIA

G. brachycera, Huckleberry, comes from eastern North America and is low-growing, with leathery dark leaves. It has white flowers in early summer, grows in sun or shade, and is tolerant of fairly dry conditions.

GRISELINIA

G. littoralis is often grown as a hedge or windbreak in coastal areas, but it also does well in light woodland. It can reach 20 feet (6 metres) but is usually less. It grows in any soil but can be damaged by frost in cold areas. The flowers are inconspicuous; it is grown as a foliage plant. The leaves are round, shiny and a very bright green. 'Variegata' has leaves variegated white. 'Dixon's Cream' is one of the finest of all variegated plants. The leaves are irregularly blotched with large splashes of creamy white. It comes from New Zealand.

G. lucida is another New Zealand species, but is much less hardy. It has large, very glossy leaves and looks very handsome.

HYPERICUM

This is an important garden genus whose members produce yellow flowers over a long period in summer and autumn. Most are not fussy about soil and will grow in sun or part shade. Many of the species are really semi-evergreen, as some leaves are lost in winter; the colder it is, the more leaves are lost.

H. calycinum, the Rose of Sharon, is one of the most useful of all ground-cover plants for difficult areas. It is one of the few that will grow well in dry shade, and it is often used to cover dry banks. In more favourable conditions, it is apt to become invasive. It grows to about a foot (30 cm) tall and has large, golden flowers with prominent stamens

Hypericum 'Hidcote'

borne over a long period in summer. 'Hidcote', believed to be a hybrid of unknown origin, is a splendid plant with yellow flowers about 3 inches (7 cm) across borne freely through summer until autumn. It can grow 4 or 5 feet (up to 1·5 metres) tall and as much across. If it gets too large, it can be cut back in spring.

H. hookeranum is smaller, with blue-green leaves and paler yellow flowers from late summer on. It comes from Nepal, India and Burma.

H. × inodorum (*H. androsaemum × H. hircinum*) has small flowers; its chief attraction is the red fruit. 'Elstead' is a particularly good form with fruits of bright coral red. It grows about 4 feet (1·2 metres) tall.

H. × moseranum (*H. calycinum × H. patulum*) is usually less than 2 feet (60 cm) tall, with arching red stems and flowers 2 inches (5 cm) across with red anthers, borne from mid-summer until autumn. It can be used in similar situations to *H. calycinum*. 'Tricolor' has leaves variegated with white and tinged with red, but seems less hardy than the typical variety.

H. uralum has arching branches with small leaves, giving a ferny effect. The pale yellow flowers are smallish, but freely produced from late summer to autumn. In the wild, it is found in the Himalayas, Thailand and Sumatra. 'Rowallane' is a tall, handsome hybrid, reaching about 6 feet (2 metres) with large, cup-shaped yellow flowers. Unfortunately, it is suitable only for mild areas.

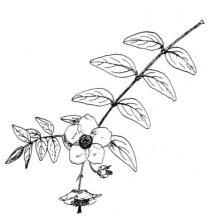

Hypericum uralum

ILEX

A large genus, some members of which look very different from the usual idea of a holly. Most grow in sun or shade, and some are tolerant of really dense shade. They are usually grown for their decorative berries, and as most species are dioecious—that is, male and female flowers are borne on different plants —it is necessary to plant both male and female forms, unless it is known that a male is within easy reach in someone else's garden.

I. × altaclarensis. A number of commonly grown cultivars are included here. 'Camelliifolia' is a handsome variety with a pyramidal habit of growth and large, glossy leaves that are mostly spineless. It has large, red berries. 'Camelliifolia Variegata' has leaves margined with yellow. 'Golden King', in spite of its name, is a female form. It has leaves with few spines, broadly edged with gold.

'Hodginsii' is a vigorous male form, with purple stems.

I. aquifolium is the common holly, native to Britain and much of Europe as well as North Africa. They grow well in sun or shade and are tolerant of atmospheric pollution. Left unclipped, they will form large shrubs or even small trees. A great many clones are available, of which I can mention only a few.

'Bacciflava' has yellow berries, freely produced.

'Golden Queen' is, strange to say, a male form, with leaves edged with yellow and shaded grey.

'Green Pillar' is a female form with an upright habit.

'Ovata Aurea'—a male form with a compact habit, gold-bordered leaves and purple twigs.

'Pyramidalis' is a free-fruiting female clone with a pyramidal growth habit. 'Pyramidalis Fructoluteo' has yellow fruits.

'Silver Queen'—another male form, with leaves edged with white.

I. corallina is a slightly tender Chinese species with long narrow leaves that are toothed, not spiny.

I. glabra, Inkberry, is a hardy, compact shrub from the eastern United States with small, glossy leaves and black berries. It dislikes lime, and tolerates dense shade.

I. latifolia is a large, handsome species from Japan, with glossy, laurel-like leaves and red berries. It is best in a sheltered situation and can tolerate deep shade.

I. opaca, American Holly, is another native of the eastern United States that dislikes a chalky soil. It is a large, spiny shrub with olive-green leaves and red berries. 'Xanthocarpa' is a form with yellow berries.

ILLICIUM

This is an interesting genus of aromatic evergreens, related to Magnolia, which like moist, acid, humus-rich soil and a sheltered situation—conditions similar to rhododendrons. There are about forty-two species, although few are seen in cultivation, mostly from south-east Asia but some from North and Central America. They can be grown against a shaded wall.

I. anisatum is a large shrub or sometimes a small tree with yellow, many-petalled flowers in spring. The leaves are fleshy, dark, glossy and scented. It comes from Formosa and Japan, where it is often planted in cemeteries and round temples.

I. floridanum, the Aniseed Tree, grows 6–10 feet (2–3 metres) tall. It has dark, leathery, oval leaves and deep crimson, nodding flowers, about 2 inches (5 cm) across, in axillary clusters. The new growth is pink. It comes from the southern USA.

I. henryi is a medium-sized Chinese species, with bright crimson-pink flowers in late spring/early summer.

JUNIPERUS

J. × media 'Pfitzerana' is the best of the prostrate junipers for a shaded situation. It is a wide-spreading shrub that can be used on its own, for its interesting shape or to hide something like a man-hole cover, or with other specimens as ground cover, as I have already described. 'Pfitzerana Aurea' has golden colouring—I do not know how well this lasts in shade—and 'Pfitzerana Glauca' has grey-blue leaves.

KALMIA

The leaves are rhododendron-like (both genera belong to the Ericaceae) and the plants need similar conditions, that is, humus-rich, acid soil and partial shade. They need a certain amount of sun if they are to flower freely. All are natives of North America.

K. angustifolia, from the eastern States, is known as the Sheep Laurel, perhaps because it is poisonous to grazing animals. It has pinkish-red flowers in summer, grows about 3 feet (a metre) tall and, in time, forms large clumps.

K. latifolia, the Calico Bush or Mountain Laurel, is the most widely grown species. It is usually 6–8 feet (2–2·4 metres) tall, but can reach as much as 25 feet (7·5 metres), forming a small tree. It has dark, glossy leaves, and pink, bowl-shaped flowers with darker markings in summer opening from curious domed buds.

Kalmia latifolia

'Clementine Churchill' has red flowers and 'Myrtifolia' is slow-growing and compact, with smaller leaves and flowers.

K. polifolia grows to less than 2 feet (60 cm), and has large clusters of purple-pink flowers in spring, and narrow leaves, dark and glossy above, paler below. It likes a damp situation.

KALMIOPSIS

K. leachiana is a very pretty dwarf shrub, with terminal racemes of pink flowers in spring. It is native to Oregon, and can be grown in sun or a partially shaded situation. It is a fine rock-garden plant if it can be given a position with damp, peaty soil.

LEDUM

Dwarf, ericaceous evergreens that like an acid, moist, shaded situation.

L. groenlandicum, Labrador Tea, comes from North America and Greenland. It has an upright growth habit and can reach 3 feet (a metre). It has neat, attractive foliage and white flowers in terminal clusters

Kalmiopsis leachiana

from late spring to mid-summer. 'Compactum' is about half the height and has smaller clusters of flowers.

L. palustre is a rare British native, also found elsewhere in northern Europe, Asia and America. It has clusters of white flowers at the end of the stems in late spring. The leaves are narrow, brown underneath, with recurved margins.

LEUCOTHOE

Yet another ericaceous genus liking lime-free soil and a shaded site.

L. davisiae, from California, has dark, glossy leaves and clusters of white, lily-of-the-valley-like flowers in summer. It is about 3 feet (a metre) tall and spreads by underground stems.

L. fontanesiana, which used to be called *L. catesbei*, has arching stems 4 or 5 feet (1·5 metres) tall, with short racemes of white, urn-shaped flowers along their length in late spring/early summer. It will tolerate dense shade. The leathery leaves turn red or bronze in autumn. 'Nana' is lower-growing; 'Rainbow' has leaves variegated with cream, pink and yellow.

L. keiskei is a small-growing Japanese species, with arching stems and pendant racemes of round, white flowers in summer.

LIGUSTRUM

The privets are rather a despised group of plants, but they can be handsome, particularly when allowed to grow naturally, and also are useful in that they grow in any soil and situation. They are tolerant of atmospheric pollution.

L. japonicum, Japanese Privet, must have at least partial shade and will grow in dense shade. It is a compact shrub reaching about 8 or 9 feet (2·5 metres), with glossy, rather camellia-like foliage and white flowers in late summer. It is grown in western North America, Australia and Britain.

L. lucidum, Glossy Privet, is sometimes planted as a street tree in warm areas, but is more often seen as a large shrub with leaves up to 5 inches (12·5 cm) long and white flowers in late summer. It will stand more sun than the last species but is better in shade. It comes from China.

L. ovalifolium, from Japan, is the species generally used for hedging, with smallish leaves that may be shed in a cold winter. It has white flowers in late summer that are sometimes described as fragrant, but I think the smell is horrid. 'Argenteum' has leaves bordered with white and 'Aureum' is the golden privet with leaves that are often vivid yellow. It makes a most attractive shrub if left unpruned.

LOMATIA

These are exotic-looking evergreens from Chile and Australasia. None is very hardy, but some seem less tender than was originally believed. They dislike chalk and appreciate shade.

L. ferruginea is a large shrub or a tree to perhaps 30 feet (9 metres) with ferny leaves and furry, russet stems and racemes of red and yellow flowers in summer. In Britain, it does well in mild areas like Cornwall and as far up the west coast as Inverewe in Ross and Cromarty.

L. hirsuta, like the last species, comes from Chile and seems reasonably hardy if given shelter, preferably in woodland. It is a large shrub with big, leathery leaves and creamy white flowers in late spring/early summer.

L. myricoides is an Australian species that forms a spreading shrub up to 6 feet (2 metres) tall. It has long, narrow leaves and scented, white spiky flowers.

L. tinctoria, from Tasmania, grows to only about 2 feet (60 cm) and suckers freely. It has terminal racemes of cream flowers opening from yellow buds.

LONICERA

The shrubby honeysuckles are mostly deciduous but there are a couple of shade-tolerant evergreens.

L. nitida is a rather uninspiring plant, but is useful for hedging in shaded areas. It is a dense-twigged bush with very small leaves that stands clipping well. 'Baggesen's

Gold' has leaves that are yellow in summer, and turn greener in autumn and winter.

L. pileata is semi-evergreen rather than fully evergreen. It grows 2 or 3 feet (up to a metre) high, but has a spread of about three times that. Its small leaves are vivid green and it is useful for planting on a shady bank.

MAHONIA

This is a large genus of about fifty species that used to be classed with *Berberis*, but although the flowers are similar (and always yellow), the leaves are very different. The Mahonias have pinnate leaves, sometimes very large, and these form a large part of their attraction.

M. acanthifolia is one of the most striking species, making a large shrub or even a small tree, with very long, pinnate leaves and scented yellow flowers in autumn and winter. Unfortunately it can only be grown in mild areas. It is a native of Nepal and neighbouring states.

M. aquifolium, the Oregon Grape, is a most useful small shrub from western North America that seems to grow in any situation including dense, dry shade. In Britain it rarely grows more than about 4 feet (1·2 metres) high, but in its native area can be considerably taller. It has pinnate leaves usually with five to nine leaflets and dense heads of scented yellow flowers in spring, followed by blue-purple berries. The glossy leaves sometimes turn bronze or red in winter.

M. bealei is a fairly large shrub from China with erect racemes of yellow scented flowers in early spring and stiff, pinnate leaves almost 18 inches (45 cm) long. It too tolerates dense shade.

M. japonica is similar to the last species, but much commoner in cultivation. It differs in flowering earlier, throughout winter, and in having pendulous instead of upright racemes. Both this and the last species are plants of considerable architectural value as long as they are given sufficient room.

M. lomariifolia, from Yunnan, is another species for a mild area. It is tall and sometimes tree-like, and has long leaves with up to nineteen pairs of narrowish leaflets. The flowers are in dense, erect racemes, opening in winter.

'Charity' is a very handsome hybrid between the last two species, rather intermediate in appearance but hardier than *M. lomariifolia*. This and the last three species look equally well in woodland or a town garden.

M. nervosa is a dwarf species, rather similar to *M. aquifolia* but only growing to 18 inches or 2 feet (45–60 cm). It also comes from the west United States.

NANDINA

N. domestica is a graceful shrub growing to about 5 feet (1·5 metres) tall, with ferny leaves that turn red in autumn and terminal panicles of fluffy white flowers in late summer. In Britain, it likes a sheltered position, moist but with good drainage, and with plenty of sun, but in areas where the summer is hotter, such as the Pacific coast of America and Australia, it does better with partial shade. It is a native of India, central China and Japan. 'Nana Purpurea' is more compact, with purplish leaves.

OSMANTHUS

O. armatus is a large, handsome shrub with spiny leaves rather like a holly's, but 6 or 7 inches (about 16 cm) long. It has scented white flowers in autumn and will grow in any situation, from sun to quite dense shade. It comes from west China.

O. delavayi has small, dark, glossy leaves with slightly toothed edges and clusters of small, scented, white, long-tubed flowers in spring. Oddly enough, the perfume of the flowers seems to be more noticeable at a slight distance than at close quarters. It forms a dense bush 6–8 feet (2–2·4 metres) tall and as much or more across. It is an attractive plant and, although it is supposed not to be hardy in cold areas, will grow in the north of England, given some

Osmanthus delavayi

shelter. It is widely grown in Australia and does well along the west coast of the United States.

O. heterophyllus (*ilicifolius*) has leaves very much like a holly's, but opposite instead of alternate and usually smaller. The small, scented flowers open in autumn, and it grows in sun or light shade. A number of forms are available, including 'Aureomarginatus', with leaves bordered with yellow, and 'Variegatus', which has leaves edged with white.

O. yunnanensis is a shrub or tree growing about 20 feet (6 metres) high, with lanceolate dark green leaves up to 9 inches (22·5 cm) long. It looks exotic, but seems reasonably hardy. Unfortunately the flowers are

Osmanthus yunnanensis

much less splendid, being small and white with a curious scent.

× OSMAREA

'Burkwoodii' is a bigeneric hybrid between *Osmanthus delavayi* and *Phillyrea decora*. It is rather similar in effect to the former, but is larger and hardier. It has scented white flowers in late spring.

× *Osmarea* 'Burkwoodii'

PACHISTIMA

P. canbyi is a dwarf, spreading shrub less than a foot (30 cm) tall, with small, dark green leaves and in-conspicuous greenish flowers follow-ed by white fruit. It will grow in sun or shade. It comes from the moun-tains of Virginia and is very hardy.

P. myrsinites, the False Box from west North America, is slightly taller, growing to about 18 inches (45 cm), and is useful in that it tolerates really

dense shade. The flowers are very small, but the small, dark, leathery leaves are quite attractive. Neither of these species likes chalk.

PACHYSANDRA

These little sub-shrubs will grow with some lime in the soil, but will not tolerate chalk.

P. terminalis grows about 9 inches (22·5 cm) high, with toothed leaves clustered at the ends of the stems and terminal racemes of greenish-white flowers in early spring. It is a most useful ground-cover plant, particularly under trees, as it will grow in dense shade where few other plants will, provided there is sufficient moisture. It is used much more widely in the United States than in Britain or Australia. It comes from Japan and is very hardy.

Pachysandra terminalis

P. axillaris is a Chinese species that can be used in the same way, but does not spread to the same extent.

P. procumbens, from the S. E. United States, is more semi-evergreen. It has spikes of greenish-white flowers in spring.

PERNETTYA

Small, ericaceous shrubs that dislike lime. All have white flowers; the berries (for which they are grown) remain on the plant over-winter, if not eaten by birds. I am including them here because they do grow well in shade, but they are better with quite a lot of sun as they flower and fruit more freely and the habit is more compact.

P. buxifolia is a Mexican species, that forms a low mound. The berries are large, white or pale pink.

P. leucocarpa is dwarf and compact, with white berries. It comes from Chile. 'Harold Comber' is a form with large, deep pink berries.

P. mucronata is the most commonly grown species. It is very hardy and suckers freely, making large clumps about 2 feet (60 cm) high. The small, glossy leaves are slightly prickly. Usually several plants need to be close together to ensure berry production, as it is partly dioecious. The berries are large and round, varying in colour from white to purple, according to the variety. It too comes from Chile. 'Bell's Seedling' has large, dark red berries and red young stems. It is supposed to be hermaphrodite, and to produce berries on its own, but in my experience it does not do so freely. 'Davis's Hybrids' have large berries in a variety of colours. 'Lilacina' has lilac-pink berries, borne profusely. 'Seashell' has pink berries, deepening as they ripen and 'White Pearl' has large white berries. 'Thymifolia' is a small, neat male form.

P. prostrata is a prostrate, Chilean species with black-purple berries; 'Pentlandii' is more vigorous, with larger fruit.

P. pumila, again from Chile, is very tiny but spreads rapidly, forming a good ground cover in sun or shade. Its berries are white, sometimes tinged with pink.

P. tasmanica is a Tasmanian species that grows only a couple of inches high, with very small leaves and red berries.

PHYLLODOCE

Dwarf, ericaceous shrubs that need a moist, lime-free, peaty but well-drained soil. In cool areas like Scotland and the north of England, they like an open, sunny site, but do better in light shade in places with a sunnier climate.

P. aleutica comes from Kamchatka and northern Japan. It grows about 10 inches (25 cm) high and has clusters of creamy yellow urn-shaped flowers in early summer.

P. breweri, from California, has rosy-purple, saucer-shaped flowers in early summer.

P. caerulea is a very rare British native, with purple, urn-shaped flowers in early summer.

P. nipponica grows about a foot (30 cm) tall, and has white or pink, bell-shaped flowers in late spring/early summer.

PIERIS

Yet another member of the Ericaceae, but not a dwarf. Like most of its relatives, this genus likes a moist, acid soil with plenty of humus and a shaded position. All the species in cultivation are evergreen and have panicles of urn-shaped white or creamy-white flowers. These are formed in autumn and the buds remain dormant until about mid-spring—sometimes they are lost in a cold winter.

P. floribunda, which comes from the south-east USA, is probably the hardiest. It grows 5 or 6 feet (about 1·5 metres) tall, in a dense mound. The flowers open in spring. Var. *elongata* has longer panicles and flowers slightly later.

P. formosa var. *forrestii* is without doubt the gem of the genus. It has the usual, white, lily-of-the-valley-like flowers, scented and in drooping panicles; what makes it so outstanding is the spectacular red young growth, as vivid as a scarlet geranium. Although the plant itself is hardy enough, both the young growth and the flowers may be caught by spring frosts. However, it

Pieris formosa var. *forrestii*

makes more new growth later to replace what is lost, and often has a second flush in autumn—which, of course, may be lost to early frosts! It grows usually about 10 feet (3 metres) tall but I have seen many tree-like specimens that must have been twice that size. It was collected by George Forrest in Yunnan and Upper Burma. 'Wakehurst' is a vigorous form with broader leaves and 'Jermyns' is a clone where the flower-stalks and sepals are the same rich red as the new leaves.

P. japonica also grows to 10 feet (3 metres) or more—I have seen some very large bushes in sheltered areas. The flowers again open in spring, in drooping panicles. The young growth is copper-bronze. There are a number of garden varieties—'Blush' has pink flowers, and 'Christmas Cheer' is a very free-flowering form with pink-tipped petals which has become available in Australia in the last year or so. 'Variegata' has leaves edged with silver, tinged pink when young. The leaves are smaller than in the typical form and it is much slower-growing—in fact, I assumed it remained a dwarf until I saw a specimen recently that must have been 8 feet (2·4 metres) tall. This variety does not seem to flower.

Pieris japonica

P. taiwanensis is similar to *P. japonica* but is more compact and has larger flowers and leaves.

PRUNUS

Most members of this genus, such as the Cherries, are sunloving, but the laurels are very shade-tolerant.

P. laurocerasus, the Cherry Laurel, still seems to bear the aura of Victoran shrubberies and is rather unjustly despised. It is tolerant of dense shade and even drip from trees, and is most often seen as a hedge, but it looks most impressive when allowed to grow freely, developing into a shrub 25 feet (7·5 metres) or so high with graceful spreading branches. It has upright spikes of fluffy white flowers in late spring, followed by black berries. There are a number of cultivars: 'Magnoliifolia' has very large, broad leaves—over a foot (30 cm) long. 'Otto Luyken' is an attractive, dwarf cultivar with a fairly upright growth habit; as the flowers are almost the same size as on the typical form, their effect is more showy.

P. lusitanicus, the Portugal Laurel, has smaller leaves than the Cherry Laurel, more pointed and darker and less glossy, with reddish stalks. If unpruned, it grows into a very large shrub or even a sizeable tree. The flowers are similar to those of the last species, but slightly smaller, and open in summer.

RAPHIOLEPIS

Evergreen shrubs that will grow in full sun or in partial shade. They like good drainage.

R. indica has narrow leaves and racemes of white, pink-tinged flowers in spring and summer. It is more tender than the next species, but does well in warmer climates.

R. umbellata is not suitable for a cold district but does well in the south of

England, the Pacific coast of the United States and Australia. It grows 3 or 4 feet (about a metre) high with a rounded habit and has slightly fleshy leaves and scented white flowers in summer, followed by black fruit. It comes from Japan and Korea.

Raphiolepis umbellata

RHODODENDRON
See also pp. 27 and 92.

A wealth of species and hybrids is included in this genus, but it is possible to mention here only a small selection of what is available. The most widely grown and most readily available rhododendrons are what are called the 'Hardy Hybrids'. For parts of the world where it is either very hot in summer or very cold in winter, or both, these are still the best as they are much more resistant to climatic extremes than the choicer varieties. Besides this, they are very

free-flowering, but the form of the flowers tends to be similar and the foliage is usually rather nondescript. Also, most grow pretty large—too much so for a small garden. For most parts of the British Isles and New Zealand, for the Pacific coast of America and favoured parts of Australia such as the Melbourne area, there are many other species and hybrids that are much more interesting and no more difficult to grow.

Hardy Hybrids

I have divided the flowering season into early (E)—spring; mid (M)—late spring and early summer; late (L)—mid-summer on.

'Alice'—tall, large pink flowers (M).
'Bagshot Ruby'—rich red flowers with some brown spotting (M–L).
'Betty Wormald'—large pink flowers with red spotting opening from red buds (M).
'Blue Peter'—vigorous but fairly compact; lilac flowers with dark eye, very free-flowering (M).
'Britannia'—low-growing and compact; brilliant red flowers but rather yellow-green foliage (M).
'C. B. van Nes'—scarlet flowers; medium sized (E).
'Christmas Cheer'—pale pink flowers opening from darker buds; compact and low-growing, very early.
'Countess of Athlone'—pale lilac flowers opening from darker buds; medium growth (M).

'Cunningham's White'—extremely hardy and reputedly good in industrial areas; white flowers from lilac buds (M).

'Cynthia'—also very hardy, and grows very large, with brilliant magenta flowers (M).

'Doncaster'—dark red flowers and dark, glossy leaves; low-growing and compact (M). Does not stand heat too well.

'Dr Stocker'—white flowers marked with red (E–M).

'Fatsuosum Flore Pleno'—double violet flowers, very long-lasting; medium growth (L).

'Gomer Waterer'—dense growth and dark, glossy leaves; tight trusses of lilac-tinged white flowers with a yellow blotch opening from lilac buds (L).

'Ivery's Scarlet'—tall, with bright red flowers and long, narrow leaves; stands heat well (E).

'Jacksonii' — medium-sized, slow-growing; bright pink flowers with purple markings; very early and tolerant of pollution.

'Lady Clementine Mitford'—large grower with good foliage; peach-pink flowers with small yellow eye (M–L).

'Loder's White'—very free-flowering, with large, conical trusses of white flowers opening from pink buds (M–L).

'Lord Roberts'—tight trusses of dark red flowers with a black blotch; medium and compact growth (M–L).

'Moser's Maroon'—tall and vigorous with maroon flowers with dark markings and reddish young growth (M–L).

'Mount Everest'—large, conical trusses of white flowers speckled in throat (E).

'Mrs Furnival'—pink flowers with dark brown eye (M–L).

'Mrs G. W. Leak'—bright pink flowers with red blotch, medium growth (M).

'Nobleanum'—slow-growing, very early. There are three colour forms: 'Album' is white; 'Coccineum' is rich, deep pink; 'Venustum' is paler pink and is the earliest-flowering of all.

'Old Port'—red-purple flowers with black markings, glossy foliage, vigorous grower (M–L).

'Pink Pearl'—one of the most widely planted of all rhododendrons; very large, rather frilly pink flowers; large, rather open growth (M).

'Royal Purple'—deep purple flowers with yellow eye; large, with narrow leaves (L).

'Sappho'—conical trusses of white flowers with a purple blotch; large, vigorous grower (M).

'White Pearl'—very hardy and stands exposure; pale pink flowers that fade to white, speckled with red in throat (M).

Species

R. aberconwayi is relatively new to cultivation; the first seeds were sent to England in 1937. It grows to about 4 feet (1·2 metres), is very hardy and does well in drier areas. It has large, saucer-shaped pink or white flowers in late spring/early summer.

R. augustinii can reach 15 feet (4·5 metres) in height, but with its willowy leaves it never looks bulky or over-powering and is fairly slow-growing. The flowers are large and wide open, often in groups of three, and in the best forms are a marvellous, lumin-ous violet-blue, sometimes with red stamens. Other forms are more lavender-coloured, but all are ex-tremely free-flowering. Some forms are less hardy than others.

R. bureavii is one of the finest of all foliage species, growing about 8 feet (2·4 metres) high, with dark green leaves with a rusty-red indumentum below. The flowers are not particu-larly striking but pleasant enough, pink or white in a tight truss, open-ing in spring.

R. calostrotum rarely grows to more than 3 feet (a metre). It has neat, grey-green leaves and rosy-purple, wide-open flowers in early summer. It dislikes a hot, dry situation. Its relative *R. radicans* is quite prostrate, with tiny leaves about ½ inch (1 cm) long and relatively large, purple flowers.

R. campylocarpum is one of the best yellow-flowered rhododendrons. It has large, bell-shaped flowers in late spring; it usually grows to about 5 feet (1·5 metres), but var. *elatum* is taller, with orange buds.

R. campylogynum is a very distinctive species; the typical variety grows about 2 feet (60 cm) tall and has

flowers like little hanging thimbles, about ¾ inch (2 cm) long, in late spring/early summer. Different forms may be taller or smaller, and the colour of the flowers varies from salmon to dusky pink, rose or purple. No garden is so small that it does not have room for this.

R. ciliatum is a lovely plant with pale pink, scented flowers and glossy dark leaves fringed with hairs. It flowers in spring, and so must have as frost-free a position as possible.

R. cinnabarinum is a tall species with long, hanging tubular flowers whose colour varies from orange-yellow to purple, depending on the form. It has lovely, rounded, blue-grey foliage and a graceful habit. It needs a bit of shelter. The flowering time is usually late spring/early summer.

R. concatens is closely related to the last species; indeed it may be a form of it. It is smaller, with yellow flow-ers and very blue new growth.

R. crassum has glossy leaves with a rather succulent appearance, and large, white, scented flowers in summer. Some forms are tender, but others seem quite hardy.

R. davidsonianum is rather like *R. augustinii*, but the flowers are pink and not so large. Again, they are borne in great profusion, in late spring.

R. edgeworthii (*R. bullatum*) has large, heavily scented, white, pink-tinged flowers opening in late spring, and distinctive leaves with deeply impressed veins. It is not hardy enough for a cold area, but I have seen it growing well in gardens in the south of England and western Scotland. Like other slightly tender species, it does very well in Australia. It is rather a straggling grower, reaching 6–8 feet (2–2·4 metres) in height.

R. *elliottii* grows about 12 feet (3·6 metres) tall and has flowers (open in early summer) that are possibly the brightest red of any rhododendron. Unfortunately it is none too hardy, and can only be grown out of doors in the south and west of Britain, the southern Pacific coast of the USA and most of Australia and New Zealand.

R. *fargesii* and the very similar R. *oreodoxa* are very free-flowering, with lilac bells in spring which, of course, are liable to frost damage. They are best, for this reason, in a sheltered position such as light woodland. The plants themselves are hardy enough—as far north as New York in the States.

R. *formosum* has unusual striped flowers—white, flushed with pink and yellow, and with red stripes on the outside of the funnel-shaped flowers. I have seen this growing in woodland in western Scotland, but there are not many places in Britain where it can be grown successfully outside.

R. *fulvum* is a superb foliage plant that grows to about 20 feet (6 metres)

sometimes forming a small tree. The leaves have an orange-brown indumentum below that is displayed when they are blown by the wind. It has large, round trusses of pink flowers in spring.

R. *griersonianum* is another red species which I have found perfectly hardy, although it is not generally considered to be so. It has elegant, long-tubed flowers of a soft, geranium red in summer, and narrow, pointed leaves. It grows rather loosely to about 4 feet (1·2 metres).

R. *haematodes* is compact, with brilliant red flowers in early summer, and dark, pointed leaves with a brown indumentum. It is very hardy, and an excellent garden plant.

R. *impeditum* is one of a group of very similar species, mostly low-growing with starry violet flowers and small leaves. They are high alpine plants and in the wild would be covered in winter by a thick blanket of snow. In cooler areas, such as Scotland and the north of England, they are best with more or less full exposure, but in sunnier parts are better with part shade, although not directly under trees, as they dislike heat and drought. R. *impeditum* flowers in late spring. R. *fastigiatum* is slightly taller, reaching perhaps 3 feet (a metre). R. *russatum* has rich purple flowers, sometimes with a white throat and leaves slightly larger than most of its relatives—about 1 inch (2·5 cm) long—rusty-red underneath. R. *scintillans* at its best has almost royal blue flowers. *R. chryseum* is unusual in this group as it has yellow flowers; it sets off the other lavender-mauve species very well.

R. johnstoneanum is a slightly tender species related to *R. ciliatum*, with creamy-yellow, red-spotted flowers in late spring/early summer. There is a double form with white flowers called 'Double Diamond'.

R. kyawii is a magnificent, tall-growing species related to *R. elliottii* with bright green leaves and brilliant scarlet flowers that are particularly useful in opening in mid- to late summer, when most rhododendrons have finished. It does well in Australia, but unfortunately is too tender for all but the mildest parts of Britain.

R. leucaspis is hardy in all but very cold districts, but flowers in early spring so the flowers are always at risk from frost in Britain, although not in Australia and New Zealand. It is a very attractive species, with large, white, wide-open flowers with brown anthers and furry leaves.

R. makinoi is a plant one does not see very often; I cannot think why, as it is hardy and has a most striking appearance with almost linear leaves, about 7 inches (17·5 cm) long and less than 1 inch (2·5 cm) wide, and clear pink flowers in early summer. The new growth comes very late, in late summer/early autumn, and is covered with white or brown wool. This late growth is a disadvantage in colder areas, as it may not have time to ripen before the onset of winter.

R. moupinense is a beautiful early species, flowering in early spring like *R. leucaspis*. The flowers are relatively large, white or occasionally pink, and the leaves are dark and glossy, bronze when young. It rarely grows larger than 4 feet (1·2 metres) tall.

R. neriiflorum can grow up to 9 feet (2·7 metres), with a fairly spreading habit, but is usually less and is slow-growing. The flowers are brilliant scarlet with a thick, fleshy texture so that they last well, in loose clusters of about half a dozen, and are produced in late spring. The leaves are about 4 inches (10 cm) long, bright green above and white below. The sub-species *euchaites* is taller, usually with a more upright habit and slightly larger flowers.

R. nuttallii is considered to have the largest flowers of any rhododendron in cultivation—5 or 6 inches (12–15 cm) long, funnel-shaped, scented, pale yellow or white flushed with yellow and pink, in clusters of three to nine. The leaves are also attractive, bullate above and purplish in the new growth. It does well in Australia, but unfortunately it is too tender to be grown outside in Britain. It grows very large, with rather a straggling habit.

R. orbiculare is a very distinctive species, with almost round, bright green leaves and trusses of large, bright pink, bell-shaped flowers in late spring/early summer.

R. oreotrephes is a tall species with white, mauve or pink flowers, very freely produced. The foliage is as valuable as the flower, as it is a glaucous, grey-blue-green. In a cold winter, some of the leaves may be lost.

R. pemakoense is a dwarf, free-flowering species that unfortunately often has its large, lilac, funnel-shaped flowers damaged by frost as they open in mid-spring. Its close relative, *R. imperator*, opens a few weeks later and so is probably a better bet.

R. souliei is one of the few species that do better in the drier, eastern areas of Britain. It has beautiful saucer-shaped white or pink flowers in late spring/early summer and

round, bright green leaves. It grows quite large, up to about 12 feet (3·6 metres).

R. tephropeplum has almost tubular pink flowers and willow-shaped leaves, dark green above and white below. It flowers in spring and is rather bud-tender, but is a very attractive species for areas with mild winters.

R. wardii is a large, rather sprawling shrub with almost round leaves and saucer-shaped, bright yellow flowers.

R. williamsianum is a low-growing, spreading species that sometimes reaches about 5 feet (1·5 metres) in height, especially if grown in woodland. It has small, round leaves that are copper-bronze as they unfold

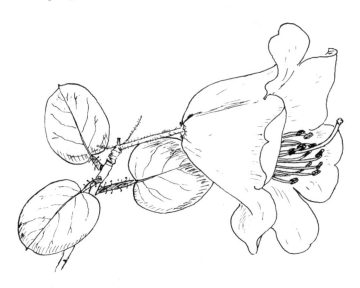

Rhododendron williamsianum

and large, pink, bell-shaped flowers. It is a very beautiful plant that seems to me hardier than it is often given credit for.

R. yakushimanum is a species that has recently become very popular in all countries where rhododendrons are grown. It is compact and slow-growing, with narrow leaves and woolly new growth, and large, round trusses of white flowers opening from pink buds in late spring/early summer. It seems tolerant of both heat and cold. A mature plant is very floriferous. Recently, it has been used a lot in hybridisation, but none of the progeny I have seen has been nearly as attractive as the parent.

R. yunnanense is a species that will tolerate more exposure than most. It is exceptionally free-flowering, with wide-open pink or white flowers, sometimes with a yellow throat, in late spring/early summer. It is a tall, open plant with willowy leaves.

Dwarf Hybrids

Many of the following are very suitable for town gardens where they will be shaded, but not actually under trees, for a large part of the day. For the sake of space I am not giving the parentage; anyone who is interested can find this information in a specialist book on rhododendrons or a catalogue from a specialist nursery.

'Alison Johnstone'—tubular, apricot-pink flowers and neat oval leaves and a graceful growth habit. Late spring/ early summer.

'Blue Bird'—one of a number of free-flowering hybrids with starry, violet-blue flowers. This one is a really vivid colour and is low-growing. Late spring.

'Blue Diamond' is rather similar but taller — it can reach 5 feet (1·5 metres)—but has a narrow habit and is not bulky-looking.

'Bow Bells' is a *R. williamsianum* hybrid, with the typical rounded leaves and low habit inherited from that parent. It has salmon-pink flowers and coppery new growth.

'Bric-a-Brac'—low-growing, with milky-white flowers with chocolate anthers in spring. There is a pink form.

Rhododendron 'Bric-a-Brac'

'Carmen' is very dwarf, with dark crimson, narrowly bell-shaped flowers, large for the size of the plant, in late spring.

'Chikor' has masses of starry primrose-yellow flowers in late spring.

'Chink' has greenish-yellow flowers
in spring and bronze new growth.

'Cilpinense' grows to about 3 feet (a
metre), with glossy, dark leaves and
scented pink flowers in spring.

'Elizabeth' is one of the best of all
hybrid rhododendrons. It can reach
4 or 5 feet (up to 1·5 metres) high,
with a fairly spreading habit, has
pointed, dark leaves and loose
trusses of large, vermilion, long-
tubed flowers in late spring, often
with a second flush in autumn.

'Jenny' is a prostrate form. This
plant seems to dislike heat and
drought—in Britain many specimens
suffered badly in the hot, dry summer of 1976.

Rhododendron 'Fabia Tangerine'

Rhododendron cilpinense

'Fabia' is another lovely plant, with
R. griersonianum as a parent in
common with the last-mentioned. It,
however, seemed very heat-resistant.
It flowers in mid-summer, with
loose trusses of orange flowers—
there are several clones, differing

slightly in colour and habit. I have
already mentioned that, although the
plant itself seems not to mind
exposure, the flowers fade quickly in
sunlight.

'Golden Horn' grows to about 4 feet
(1·2 metres) and has orange-red buds
opening to golden-orange flowers.
The clone 'Persimmon' has waxy,
scarlet flowers; both open in late
spring/early summer.

'Grayswood Pink' is compact and
very hardy; it has rounded leaves
and deep pink, bell-shaped flowers
in late spring/early summer.

'Humming Bird' is a fine williamsianum hybrid, with dark, rounded
leaves and crimson-pink flowers in
late spring/early summer. It makes
a neat mound about 4 feet (1·2
metres) high. 'Elizabeth Lockhart' is
a clone with copper-coloured foliage.
'May Day' has vivid scarlet, long-
tubed flowers and neat, pointed
leaves, brown below. It is a fine
plant; hardy, compact and free-
flowering.

'Moonshine' is also hardy and prolific, with rounded leaves and pale yellow flowers opening from pinkish buds.

'Moorheim's Scarlet' is an ultra-hardy German hybrid, low-growing, with loose trusses of deep red flowers in late spring.

'Oreocinn' is a pretty plant, with an open, twiggy habit, neat oval leaves, and trusses of pink or apricot tubular flowers, freely borne.

'Praecox' has azalea-like, lilac-pink flowers in early spring. The flowers may be frosted, but they often open over a period and so some escape. It can grow to 5 or 6 feet (1·5–2 metres) tall, but is fairly upright and is lightly built.

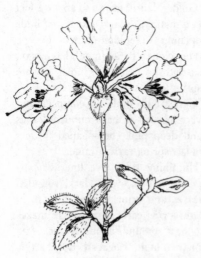

Rhododendron 'Praecox'

'St Tudy' grows to about 5 feet (1·5 metres), with an erect habit, and has intense blue-violet flowers in late spring/early summer.

'Tessa' is rather similar to 'Praecox', but slightly smaller with larger and deeper pink flowers in spring.

'Yellow Hammer' is rather a straggly grower, but it has vivid yellow, tubular flowers in spring.

Larger Hybrids

Many very beautiful plants fall into this category. Most are seen at their best in light woodland; not many are suitable for really cold areas. There may well be room for one at least in a smallish garden if a sheltered position is available.

'Albatross' is a tall shrub or even a small tree with long leaves and large trusses of scented white flowers opening from pink buds towards the beginning of summer.

'Angelo' is rather similar, again with handsome leaves and very large trusses of scented, pink-tinged white flowers in late spring/early summer.

'Avalanche' has large, white flowers with red markings inside and conspicuous red flower-stalks. 'Alpine Glow' is a form of the same cross with pink flowers.

'Carita' has trusses of large, pale yellow, bell-shaped flowers in spring. Some clones have pink flowers.

'Cinnkeys' is open in habit, with clusters of tubular orange flowers flushed with yellow in late spring/early summer and neat, oval leaves.

'Cornish Cross'—tall and open, with smooth, reddish bark and loose trusses of large, bell-shaped, deep rose-pink flowers in spring.

'Damaris'—bell-shaped, pale yellow flowers and dark, glossy foliage. 'Logan' is the best clone, with bright yellow flowers.

'Fusilier' has large trusses of vivid red, bell-shaped flowers in late spring/early summer and narrow, pointed leaves.

'Halcyone'—loose trusses of wide-open, pink flowers in late spring/early summer.

'Hawk'—clusters of yellow, bell-shaped flowers opening in late spring/early summer from apricot buds. 'Crest' and 'Jervis Bay' are two of the best clones.

'Idealist' has large, creamy flowers with a red blotch, opening from pink buds in late spring.

'Jalisco'—waxy, narrowly bell-shaped flowers in early summer; in the form 'Eclipse' they are yellow, streaked with crimson; in 'Elect' they are primrose yellow.

'Lady Bessborough'—tall, with trusses of creamy flowers from apricot buds in late spring/early summer. 'Roberte' has salmon-pink flowers.

'Lady Chamberlain' is a beautiful hybrid of R. cinnabarinum with large, waxy, pendant flowers and rounded glaucous foliage. There are a number of clones with differently coloured flowers: 'Exbury' is yellow, flushed with orange; 'Gleam' is orange-red outside and yellow inside; 'Salmon Trout' is salmon-pink and 'Seville' is orange. All flower in late spring/early summer.

'Lady Rosebery' is another cinna-barinum cross, very similar to the last and equally beautiful but with flowers in shades of pink.

'Lionel's Triumph' has large trusses of bell-shaped yellow flowers blotched with red inside, in late spring.

'Loderi' forms a large, often tree-like bush with enormous, frilly, heavily scented flowers opening in late spring/early summer. There are a number of clones; most are white although the buds are often pinkish, but 'Venus' remains pink and 'Julie' is creamy yellow.

'Naomi'—large, with trusses of wide-open, lilac flowers in late spring. 'Glow' is a clone with bright pink flowers; 'Hope' is pink, tinged with lavender; 'Nautilus' has particularly large, frilly, pink flowers; 'Stella Maris' is pale yellow, shaded pink.

'Penjerrick' is another tall hybrid, forming an open bush or a small tree, with coppery bark, good foliage and loose trusses of cream, pale yellow or pink bell-shaped flowers in late spring.

'Polar Bear' is very large, sometimes tree-like, with large leaves. It has very large trusses of scented white flowers with a greenish eye, opening late, in summer.

'Romany Chai' is another late-flowering variety, with scarlet flowers with a maroon eye, in mid-summer.

'Romany Chal' also flowers in mid-summer; it has bell-shaped, brilliant red flowers with a black blotch.

'Shilsonii' makes a large bush or a small tree with lovely smooth, reddish bark and lax trusses of bell-shaped blood red flowers in spring.

'Tally Ho' is more compact, with round trusses of bright scarlet flowers in mid-summer.

'Unique' has large trusses of creamy white flowers tinged with pink in late spring.

EVERGREEN AZALEAS

These, too, are members of the genus *Rhododendron*. Most are low-growing and free-flowering and are very suitable for town gardens. They can be grown in tubs and even window-boxes. They do better in full exposure in Scotland and the north of England, but in warmer parts need some shade, although not under trees. These plants are widely grown in all parts of the world where rhododendrons are grown at all. Again, only a small selection of the many varieties available can be mentioned here.

Kurume group

These originated in Japan and were first seen in the west at an exhibition in San Francisco in 1915. Most are low-growing and flower in late spring/early summer. The term 'hose-in-hose' means that the calyx is like the petals, so that there seems to be two flowers sitting one inside the other.

'Azuma-kagami' (Pink Pearl)—salmon pink, hose-in-hose; taller than most, up to 5 feet (1·5 metres).

'Hatsugiri'—very compact; magenta purple.

'Hino Crimson'—crimson.

'Hinodegiri' (Red Hussar)—brilliant red.

'Hinomayo'—large pink flowers; grows to 4 or 5 feet (upto 1·5 metres).

'Hoo' (Apple Blossom)—pink with white throat.

'Irohayama' (Dainty)—rosy-lavender, chestnut eye.

'Kirin' (Coral Bells or Daybreak)—rose pink with red anthers, hose-in-hose.

'Kure-no-yuki'—white, hose-in-hose.

'Vida Brown'—rose red, large flowers.

Kaempferi hybrids

Taller and larger-flowered than the kurumes, and also slightly later—opening in early summer. They are better in cooler areas than the kurumes, but many have flowers that fade badly in hot sun.

'Addy Wery'—bright red.

'Bengal Fire'—fiery red.

'Betty'—orange-pink with darker eye.

'Blaauw's Pink'—salmon pink, hose-in-hose.

'Favorite'—deep pink.

'Fedora'—large, bright pink flowers.

'Jeanette'—large pink flowers, spotted red.

'John Cairns'—brick red, tall growing, particularly good in cooler areas.

'Kathleen'—rose red.

'Louise'—salmon red.

'Naomi'—salmon pink, late.
'Orange Beauty'—orange with tinges of pink.
'Willy'—soft pink.
'Zampa'—orange red.

Vuyk hybrids

Raised in Holland and similar to the Kaempferis. Hardy, with large flowers in late spring/early summer.

'Beethoven'—magenta.
'Palestrina'—white with a green eye, bright green leaves. A lovely plant, but often reluctant to flower.
'Princess Beatrix'—orange.
'Princess Irene'—geranium red.
'Purple Triumph'—deep purple.
'Schubert'—bright pink.
'Vuyk's Rosy Red'—rose red.
'Vuyk's Scarlet'—deep red. Both this and the previous hybrid are very free-flowering.

Glenn Dale hybrids

Bred in eastern USA; most are very hardy, with large flowers.

'Ambrosia'—pink, fading to apricot.
'Challenger'—orange-red, flushed with mauve.
'Chanticleer'—purple.
'Darkness'—brick red with crimson blotch; compact.
'Elizabeth'—pink; spreading habit.
'Everest'—white, large flowers.
'Martha Hitchcock'—white with lilac edge; late.
'Merlin'—magenta pink.
'Polar Sea'—white, frilly, with green blotch.

'Tanager'—bright red, dark flare.

Gable hybrids

Also American-raised. Large flowers.

'Elizabeth Gable'—light red.
'James Gable'—red with dark blotch, hose-in-hose.
'Louise Gable'—double salmon-pink.
'Rosebud'—double pale pink.

Satsuki and Wada hybrids

Originated in Japan. These plants are very useful for their late flowering time—mid-summer—but need a warm district.

'Chichebu'—white, hose-in-hose.
'Kusudama'—magenta with white throat.
'Pink Delight'—pink.

Indian or indica hybrids

Large-flowered plants originally bred in Belgium and Britain as greenhouse and indoor pot plants. They are valuable garden plants in Australia and the United States south of Washington. Many varieties are available.

'Avenir'—brick red, double.
'Avenir Alba'—double white.
'Ballerina'—red and white.
'Elsa Karga'—double red.
'Gretel'—double; white flowers edged with cherry red.
'Leopold Astrid'—double; red edged with white.
'Peace'—double pink.

'Perle de Noisy'—double pink and white.

'Ruth Kirk'—large, single salmon pink.

Others

'Balsaminiflorum'—salmon red, double; leaves with long, white hairs.

'Chippewa'—rose pink; late-flowering.

'Fancy Gumpo'—frilly, pale pink flowers, marked with deeper pink.

'Gumpo'—white.

'Gumpo Red'—pink.

'Mother's Day'—semi-double, red.

RIBES

R. viburnifolium, Cataline Perfume, is a native of California that grows about 3 feet (a metre) tall with a greater spread. It has glossy, evergreen leaves and small red flowers. It grows in quite dense shade, even dry shade under trees, and is widely used in this way in its native state. In Britain it is hardy only in the very mildest areas.

RUBUS

Some of the ornamental brambles are grown for their flowers and others for their decorative stems.

R. calycinoides (*fockeanus*) is a dwarf, creeping evergreen, with lobed leaves covered with grey wool below. It has white flowers in summer and makes a pleasant ground-cover plant in a shaded area.

R. nutans is another low-growing, creeping evergreen with trifoliate leaves and nodding white flowers in mid-summer, followed by purple, edible fruit. It prefers a shady situation and is good for covering a bank. It comes from the Himalayas.

R. tricolor is another ground cover species with trailing stems and leaves that are dark and glossy above, white below. The white flowers are followed by red, edible fruit. This species will grow in heavy shade, even under beech trees. It comes from western China.

RUSCUS

These curious plants are adapted for living in dry places. The true leaves are reduced to scales; the leaf-like structures are in fact flattened stems —the tiny flowers are borne on the surface of these, followed, in the case of female plants, by large red berries.

R. aculeatus, Butcher's Broom, is a British native that grows wild often in dense shade, under trees, usually where it is very dry. The 'leaves' are spiny at the tip and the red berries are very showy. Both sexes must be present for these to be produced. It grows about 2 feet (60 cm) high and spreads by underground stems.

R. hypoglossum comes from southern Europe and is rather similar to the last species but with larger 'leaves'. It also grows in dense shade.

SARCOCOCCA

These are winter-flowering evergreens, sometimes known in Britain as Christmas Box, which make good ground-cover plants in shade. The flowers are rather insignificant, but the foliage is neat and attractive and useful for cutting.

S. confusa grows slowly to 3 or 4 feet (about a metre), with a spreading habit. It has glossy, pointed leaves and small, strongly scented white flowers in mid- to late winter, followed by black berries.

S. hookeranum grows to about 4 feet (1·2 metres), spreading by suckers. It will grow in dense shade; it has dark, willowy leaves and scented white flowers with pink anthers, followed by black berries. Var. *digyna* has narrower leaves and is hardier than the typical variety.

Sarcococca hookeranum var. *digyna*

S. humilis is similar but smaller. It is less than 2 feet (60 cm) tall and forms large clumps.

SCHIMA

Evergreen trees and shrubs related to Camellia, and also requiring a lime-free soil. They need a sheltered position in a mild area.

S. argentea is a large, erect shrub with glossy, dark leaves and white flowers about 2 inches (5 cm) across borne in late summer on the current year's growth. It comes from west China and Assam.

S. khasiana is a large shrub, sometimes a small tree, that again flowers on the young wood, in early autumn. The flowers are white with yellow stamens, about 2 inches (5 cm) across. The glossy, toothed leaves may be up to 8 inches (20 cm) long. It is more tender than the last species.

SKIMMIA

Evergreen shrubs grown mainly for their berries, that do well in shade, even dense shade.

S. japonica forms a dense mound, about 4 feet (1·2 metres) high and more across, with pointed, leathery leaves, and white flowers in late spring. Male and female flowers are on different plants, and the female ones are followed by red berries. A number of clones are available— 'Foremanii' is a vigorous female form with broad leaves and very large fruit clusters, and 'Rogersii' is another female clone, which is dwarf and slow-growing. Two good male forms are 'Fragrans' with scented flowers, and 'Rubella' which has red buds.

S. reevesiana, from China, is hermaphrodite, so only one plant is required for berrying. It is similar to the last species but smaller, usually less than 2 feet (60 cm) tall.

TAXUS

Yews are very accommodating plants as they grow in any soil and situation, including dense shade. They are tolerant of drought and atmospheric pollution.

T. baccata, Common Yew or English Yew, is too well known to need description. Not everyone is aware, however, that there are many cultivars available, some with golden foliage and others prostrate.

'Aurea', the Golden Yew, forms a large but compact shrub, with golden-yellow leaves that eventually turn green.

'Elegantissima' is another golden form with brighter yellow young leaves and a fairly upright habit.

'Fastigiata', the Irish Yew, has a columnar habit particularly when young.

'Repandens' is more or less prostrate and makes a fine ground-cover plant in dense shade.

'Repens Aurea' is low-growing and spreading with leaves edged with yellow. This colour is not retained if it is planted in really dense shade.

'Standishii' is slow-growing and columnar, with golden leaves.

VACCINIUM

A large genus of shrubs, both evergreen and deciduous, related to the heathers and like them requiring an acid soil. Some species are grown commerically for their fruit.

V. nummularia, from the Himalayas, is low-growing with small, glossy leaves and clusters of deep pink flowers in early summer, followed by black berries. It is hardy only in milder areas.

V. ovatum, the Evergreen Huckleberry, comes from western North America. It will grow in sun or dense shade—in the former situation, it is quite low-growing but in shade it may reach 8 feet (2·4 metres) high. It has leathery, glossy leaves, copper-coloured when young, and bell-shaped pink flowers in early summer, followed by edible purple fruit.

V. vitis-idaea, the Cowberry, is a British native found in the north and west on moors or in woods. It is small and creeping in habit, with neat, glossy leaves and bell-shaped, pale pink flowers in summer, followed by round red berries.

VIBURNUM

This is an important genus horticulturally; most are easily grown in sun or shade, although they dislike dry sites with poor soil.

V. × burkwoodii grows 8–10 feet

(2·4–3 metres) tall and has shiny leaves, brown and furry below, and clusters of white flowers opening from pink buds from late winter until late spring.

V. davidii has had awards both as a flowering and a fruiting shrub, but it is usually planted for the effect of its foliage and berries. It forms a compact dome, 2 or 3 feet (up to a metre) high and has glossy, leathery leaves with three conspicuous veins, bronze when young. The fruits are turquoise to blue in colour, but if they are to be freely produced it is necessary to have two or three plants close together. Flowers and fruit are borne more freely in sun than in shade, but it is worth growing as a foliage plant alone.

V. rhytidophyllum, the Leatherleaf Viburnum, has large, lance-shaped leaves, dark and glossy above with deeply impressed veins, grey and woolly below. It is particularly valuable for foliage effect on chalk, where the large-leaved rhododendrons cannot be grown. It is very hardy and can reach 20 feet (6 metres) in height; the foliage is more luxuriant when it is grown in shade. The clusters of flowers are a rather muddy white; if more than one specimen is grown, red fruits, turning black, are produced.

V. tinus, Laurustinus, has pointed dark leaves and heads of white flowers opening from pink buds from autumn until spring/early summer. It can grow to 15 feet (4·5 metres) high,

Viburnum tinus

with as great a spread. 'Eve Price' and 'Israel' are compact forms that are good value as the flowers are about the same size as the typical variety and, on a smaller plant, make more of an effect.

VINCA

The periwinkles are invaluable ground-cover plants for shady situations.

V. major, Greater Periwinkle, has long, trailing stems, that will hang down a bank or even scramble up through other shrubs. The leaves are glossy and pointed and the flowers are violet-blue, about 1½–2 inches (4–5 cm) across, borne over a long period starting in mid-spring or even earlier. 'Maculata' is a form whose leaves have a central yellowish blotch, less conspicuous in heavy shade; 'Variegata' has white-edged leaves.

V. minor, the Lesser Periwinkle, sometimes called Myrtle in America, forms an even denser ground cover as the trailing stems root more readily and give a neater effect. It is very similar to the last species, but smaller in all its parts. Both are too rampant to be allowed near anything choice. 'Alba' is a form with white flowers; 'Atropurpurea' has plum-coloured flowers, often with a white ring in the centre. 'Variegata' has white-variegated leaves and blue flowers; I do not think it is quite as vigorous as the typical form.

Vinca major

6

Deciduous Shrubs

ABELIOPHYLLUM

A. distichum is hardy and grows slowly to about 3 feet (a metre); it tolerates light to moderate shade. It looks rather like a small, white-flowered *Forsythia*; the scented flowers are borne along arching branches in early spring. It is a graceful plant that should be more widely grown. It comes from Korea.

Abeliophyllum distichum

ARONIA

A. arbutifolia, Red Chokeberry, is an American shrub 6–8 feet (2–2·4 metres) tall, grown mainly for its red, orange and yellow autumn colour. It will tolerate quite heavy shade, but the colouring is likely to be less vivid in that position. The small white flowers are followed by red berries that may persist throughout the winter. 'Erecta' is more compact and colours particularly well.

A. melanocarpa, Black Chokeberry, is a suckering shrub growing about 3 feet (a metre) tall whose leaves turn red, brown and orange in autumn. It has black berries.

CALLICARPA

These plants have attractive fruit, usually blue or lilac. The fruit is produced more freely when more than one plant is grown and also when they are not situated in too dense a shade.

C. bodinieri is a Chinese species growing about 6 feet (2 metres) tall, with small, lilac flowers and lilac-blue fruit; the leaves turn pinkish in autumn. The clone 'Profusion' and the variety *giraldii* do not need a pollinator.

C. dichotoma comes from China and Korea. It is smaller than the last species and has pink flowers in summer, followed by deep lilac fruit.

C. japonica grows to 5 or 6 feet (1·5–2 metres) and has pink flowers in late summer followed by round, violet fruit. Var. *angustata* is a Chinese form with leaves up to 10 inches (25 cm) long. 'Leucocarpa' has white fruit.

CEPHALANTHUS

C. occidentalis, the Button Bush,

comes from the southern United States. It has round heads of creamy flowers in late summer and does best in a damp situation.

CHAENOMELES

This genus is still best known to most people as 'Japonica'. They are beautiful and accommodating shrubs that grow in any soil, in sun or shade. They are most often seen grown against a wall—presumably because of their rather sprawling habit, not because they need protection—but they can be grown as free-standing bushes. If planted under trees they do not flower so freely. They can be pruned immediately after flowering.

C. japonica grows 4–5 feet (up to 1·5 metres) high, with orange-red flowers.

C. speciosa, from China, is the species to which most of the garden varieties belong. It is larger and more spreading than the last and flowers through spring. Many colour-forms are available:

'Cardinalis' is crimson red.

Chaenomeles speciosa

'Moerloosii' has large, pink and white flowers in dense clusters.

'Nivalis' is white, again with large flowers.

'Red Ruffles' is semi-double, red.

'Rubra Grandiflora'—large, crimson flowers.

'Simonii'—red, semi-double; low-growing.

C.×superba (*japonica×speciosa*) includes more good garden forms. They are vigorous and hardy, and tend to be slightly smaller than *C. speciosa* itself.

'Boule de Feu'—flame-coloured.

'Crimson and Gold'—crimson petals and prominent gold anthers.

'Etna'—vermilion red; low-growing.

'Hever Castle'—salmon pink.

'Knap Hill Scarlet'—bright scarlet flowers borne over a long period.

'Pink Lady'—pink from darker buds.

'Rowallane'—rich, deep red.

CHIMONANTHUS

C. praecox (*fragrans*) is a native of China that grows about 8 feet (2·4 metres) high, having creamy-yellow, scented flowers with a purple blotch in the centre, opening in late winter/ early spring. It is often grown against a wall but can be grown in the open with some shelter, as in light woodland. It needs good drainage and does well on chalk. 'Grandiflorus' has larger and deeper yellow flowers; 'Luteus' also has larger flowers than the typical form, without any purple staining, and opens slightly later.

Chimonanthus praecox (fragrans)

CLETHRA

Shrubs or small trees with long racemes of strongly scented white or cream flowers that dislike lime.

C. acuminata, from the southern United States, has one-sided racemes of white flowers in late summer and light green, pointed leaves that turn yellow in autumn. It grows up to 10 feet (3 metres) tall, with a fairly upright habit.

C. alnifolia, the Sweet Pepper Bush, is in flower from mid-summer till early autumn. It comes from east North America, and grows to about 8 or 9 feet (about 2·6 metres). 'Paniculata' is a particularly good form. 'Rosea' has pink-tinged flowers and is not quite so hardy.

C. barbinervis is a Japanese species with dark, glossy leaves and flowers rather like those of the Portugal Laurel, *Prunus lusitanica*. It is slightly smaller than *C. acuminata*.

C. delavayi is a very attractive species that is rather tender when young but becomes hardier as it gets older. In cultivation, it is usually 8–10 feet (2·4–3 metres) high, but in its native China, I believe it can reach 45 feet (13·5 metres). It has large racemes of Pieris-like flowers in late summer, and does well in light woodland.

CORNUS
See also pp. 25 and 30.

C. canadensis is a pleasant little carpeting plant growing only about 6 inches (15 cm) high, that will do well in dense shade. It has flowers surrounded by four prominent white bracts in summer, followed by red fruit.

CORYLOPSIS

These shrubs are much less often grown than their relatives the witch-hazels, but I think they are more attractive. They are hardy and easily grown, although they may suffer some damage from spring frosts. Most grow on any soil although they seem to do better without lime; a position in light woodland suits them well. The various species are rather similar: all have hanging racemes of scented, primrose yellow flowers in early spring, before the leaves unfold. The leaves are rather coarse and hazel-like and turn yellow or orange in autumn. They do well in Australia and New Zealand and the Pacific states of America.

C pauciflora has larger flowers than most species, borne singly or in racemes of two or three; the young growth is pinkish. It is a charming plant, reaching 4–6 feet (1·2–2 metres) high, but it does not grow on chalk. It is a native of Japan.

Corylopsis pauciflora

C. spicata, another Japanese species, is a spreading shrub 6–8 feet (2–2·4 metres) tall, with drooping racemes up to 6 inches (15 cm) long. The flowers have purple anthers and are a brighter yellow than most.

C. veitchiana, from China, is one of the best, with an upright rather than a spreading habit. It has dense racemes of primrose flowers with orange anthers and conspicuous yellow bud scales. The leaves are purplish when young.

C. willmottiae is usually a shrub 6–12 feet (2–4 metres) tall, but I have seen it as a tree. It is more effective as a bush, however, where the flowers can be seen at close range. It has dense racemes of flowers, 2–3 inches (5–7 cm) long, and the leaves are purplish when young. 'Spring

Corylopsis veitchiana

Purple' has rich purple new growth. It comes from west China.

COTONEASTER
See also p. 43.

C. adpressus is dwarf and spreading, with small leaves that have good red autumn colour, and bright red berries.

C. bullatus grows about 12 feet (3·6 metres) tall and has handsome, dark green leaves 4 or 5 inches (10–12·5 cm) long, with deeply impressed veins, which colour well in autumn. The white flowers are followed by clusters of large red fruit in late summer. Var. *floribundus* has larger leaves, flower clusters and fruit; var. *macrophyllus* has leaves 6 inches (15 cm) long.

C. horizontalis is probably the most widely grown of all the cotoneasters. The 'herring-bone' pattern of growth is very characteristic; it is often grown against low walls and is also good on shaded banks. The small leaves turn red in autumn and it has plentiful red berries that are, how-ever, attractive to birds. It rarely grows more than about 3 feet (a metre) tall.

Daphne mezereum

DAPHNE
See also p. 44.

D. mezereum is the familiar 'Daphne' of cottage gardens. It is a rare British native, long cultivated. The flowers open on the bare branches from late winter to mid-spring and although they can be a muddy pinkish-purple, they are a good red-purple in the best forms. It has showy red berries, which are poison-ous, although not to birds. On our plants, most of these fall off or are eaten before ripening, but I have seen bushes a blaze of scarlet in late summer. It usually grows about 4 feet (1·2 metres) tall. 'Alba' has white flowers; 'Rosea' has pink ones and 'Grandiflora' has larger flowers that start to open around mid-winter.

DEUTZIA

These are very easily grown shrubs related to Philadelphus that grow on any soil, in sun or light shade. They are usually rather shapeless, growing to 5 or 6 feet (1·5–2 metres) tall. Any pruning should be done immediately after flowering as they flower on the previous year's growth. They may suffer from late spring frosts, partic-ularly in low-lying areas. They are widely grown in Australia, New Zealand and the USA. Many species and garden varieties are available.

D. × *elegantissima* has scented pink flowers in mid-summer. The cultivar 'Fasciculata' has brighter pink flowers; 'Rosealind' has deep red flowers.

D. gracilis is a graceful species from Japan, with clusters of white, starry flowers in mid-summer.

Deutzia gracilis

D. × *hybrida* is a free-flowering, variable hybrid with many named clones. 'Joconde' is a vigorous one, with large, purplish flowers. 'Magicien' has large pink and white flowers, purplish on the outside. 'Mont Rose' has pink flowers with darker shading and is particularly free-flowering.

D. × *rosea* is more compact than most, with bell-shaped pink flowers; those of the cultivar 'Carminea' are deeper in colour.

D. setchuenensis is less hardy than the others, but I think it is the most attractive. It has a neat habit, growing to 4 or 5 feet (up to 1·5 metres), and masses of starry white flowers in late summer. It comes from China. Var. *corymbiflora*, which is sometimes offered, differs from the typical variety in only minor details and is equally good.

ENKIANTHUS
See also p. 31.

E. cernuus rubens is a Japanese species with clusters of deep red, urn-shaped flowers in late spring/early summer that grows usually 5 or 6 feet (1·5–2 metres) tall. The leaves colour richly in autumn.

E. perulatus is a neat shrub that can reach 6 feet (2 metres) or so. It has white flowers in late spring that blend pleasantly with the whorls of fresh green leaves that are unfolding at the same time. The leaves turn red in autumn. It too comes from Japan.

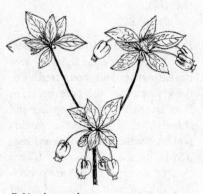

Enkianthus perulatus

FOTHERGILLA

These are attractive North American shrubs or small trees that dislike lime.

They have white or cream flower-spikes, with the stamens making the show—rather like a Bottle-brush. Most have leaves that colour well in autumn. They are widely grown in North America and Australia, but they are seen less often than might be expected in Britain.

F. gardenii is a dwarf species, growing less than 3 feet (a metre) high, with scented flowers in late spring and red autumn colour.

F. major forms a rounded bush 8–10 feet (2·4–3 metres) tall with flowers that open in spring, before the dark, glossy leaves. It has good red and yellow autumn colour.

F. monticola seems to be the most widely grown. It is very similar to the last species—the differences between them are only of botanical significance.

Fothergilla monticola

FUCHSIA

Very well-known garden plants that flourish in any good soil and in sun or shade—but not under trees. Some varieties may be grown out-of-doors in Britain; on the west coast in particular they may have a permanent woody framework, while in colder areas, the top growth is usually all cut back and the plant comes anew from the roots in spring. Other varieties, including those with very large flowers, do not survive the winter outside, but are useful for standing out in tubs during the summer, or for planting in window-boxes. In places like Australia and New Zealand where frost is not a problem, these can be left permanently outside and a shaded rather than a sunny spot is definitely to be preferred. So many of these more tender cultivars are available that it seems pointless to attempt to list them, so I shall mention only some of those that are able to withstand some frost and so may be grown outside in many places. Fuchsias are useful for the long period of colour they provide in late summer and on into autumn.

'Alice Hofman'—small, usually less than 1 foot (30 cm), with red sepals and white petals.
'Chillerton Pink'—pink calyx, lilac petals.
'Corallina'—vigorous and spreading; red sepals, purple petals.
'Dunrobin Bedder'—dwarf and spreading; red sepals, violet petals.
'Eleanor Rawlins'—very long, slightly reflexed sepals, red petals.
'Lena'—large flowers with salmon-

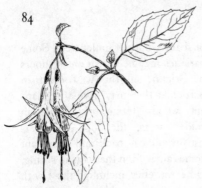

Fuchsia 'Eleanor Rawlins'

pink sepals and violet petals; 1½–2 feet (45–60 cm).
'Madame Cornelissen'—red sepals, white petals; about 2 feet (60 cm).
'Margaret' has semi-double flowers with red sepals and purple petals.

Fuchsia 'Margaret'

'Margaret Brown' — low-growing, with large flowers, crimson and red-purple.
'Marinka'—red sepals and red petals; prostrate and spreading, very good hanging over a retaining wall.
'Mrs Popple'—small, again with large flowers; red sepals and purple petals.

'Origen' is a variety with fairly ordinary red and purple flowers, but with young foliage of a vivid yellow-green that gradually darkens throughout the summer.
'Riccartonii' is similar to *F. magellanica* but even stronger growing and with broader flowers.
'Tom Thumb' is a very free-flowering dwarf cultivar with rose-red sepals and violet petals.

F. magellanica is probably the most widely grown of the hardy fuchsias; it is sometimes used for hedging in the west, where it grows 5 or 6 feet (1·5–2 metres) tall or more. The flowers are long and narrow, with a red calyx and violet petals.
'Alba' is a cultivar of this species with white flowers, tinged with violet.
Var. *gracilis* has smaller flowers than the typical form but is very free-flowering, with arching branches.

Fuchsia magellanica var. *gracilis*

'Pumila' is a dwarf form, 9–12 inches (22–30 cm) high.

'Variegata' has leaves edged with cream, with some pink.

'Versicolor' is one of the most attractive cultivars, with grey-green leaves flushed with pink and variegated with white and the usual crimson and purple flowers.

F. procumbens is a New Zealand species that does not look much like a fuchsia at all. It is dwarf and procumbent, with small, roundish leaves and yellow and purple flowers followed by red-purple berries. It is a curiosity rather than a showy plant and is only suitable for a mild area.

GAYLUSSACIA

G. baccata, the Black Huckleberry, is a shrub from eastern North America growing about 3 feet (a metre) tall, with small, reddish flowers and black fruit. It grows in dry or moist situations, in sun or light shade.

HAMAMELIS

The witch-hazels are very popular winter-flowering plants with flowers that seem quite unaffected by frost. They can be grown in a wide range of climatic conditions, but they do not like alkaline soils or heavy clay. Although they grow well in partial shade, particularly light woodland, they flower more freely in sun. Plants are often grafted on to *H. virginiana* stock and this produces suckers which should be removed. Plants on their own roots are to be preferred, but they are not too easily raised from cuttings. All the species have hazel-like leaves, usually hairy and rather coarse-looking.

H. japonica, from Japan, is usually a spreading shrub to about 12 feet (3·6 metres). It flowers at the same time as the next species and has paler yellow petals, even more narrow and twisted. 'Arborea' is taller and can be tree-like; 'Sulphurea' has pale yellow, crimped petals and 'Zuccariniana' flowers later, in mid-spring, and has very curly petals.

H. mollis, from China, is the most widely grown species, and is probably the best. It makes a large bush, sometimes as much as 20 feet (6

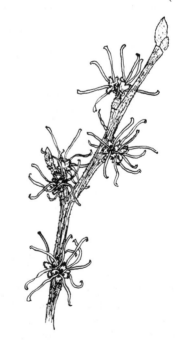

Hamamelis mollis

metres) tall. The sweetly-scented flowers with their long, spidery petals, slightly crimped at the tips, are borne on the bare wood in clusters of about four, from mid-winter to mid-spring. 'Brevipetala' has shorter petals, making the clusters seem more dense. 'Pallida' has lemon-yellow flowers.

H. × *intermedia* is a natural hybrid that arises when these two species are grown together, and flowers from late winter to mid-spring. There are a number of named clones—'All-gold' has deep yellow flowers; 'Jelena' is very vigorous, with large, orange-bronze flowers and good red and orange autumn colour; 'Ruby Glow' has reddish-bronze flowers and an erect habit.

Leaf of Hamamelis × *intermedia* 'Jelena'

H. virginiana, from the USA, grows to about 12 feet (3·6 metres). It starts to flower in early autumn, before the leaves fall, and is less showy than the others mentioned.

HOLODISCUS

H. discolor, from North America, is a tall shrub reaching about 12 feet (3·6 metres), with arching branches and long, feathery panicles of creamy flowers in summer. It is widely grown in the States, where it is sometimes called Ocean Spray, and grows in sun or part shade.

HYDRANGEA

Everyone knows the hortensia-type hydrangeas with large, round flower-heads, but these are less suitable for an informal garden than many of the lesser-grown species and hybrids, although they look well in tubs on a terrace. They grow anywhere in the British Isles, although particularly luxuriantly in the south and west. They are widely grown in Australia where they must have shelter from the hot sun.

H. aspera now includes the species formerly known as *H. sargentiana* and *H. villosa*. It has large, velvety leaves and pale blue flowers, sur-rounded by pink or white ray florets, in summer. It comes from west China and the Himalayas and grows about 8 feet (2·4 metres) tall—it looks splendid in a woodland setting. 'Ayesha' has scented flowers looking very much like a lilac's, pink or lilac in colour, and glossy leaves.

H. involucrata rarely grows taller than 3 or 4 feet (about a metre), and has blue or lilac flowers surrounded by white ray florets. 'Hortensis' is a form with double, creamy flowers that turn pinkish.

H. macrophylla includes the two most widely grown groups, the Hortensias and the Lacecaps. The former have large, round heads of sterile ray florets while the latter have flat heads of small fertile flowers surrounded by larger sterile flowers. Some forms are blue in acid soil but pink in alkaline soil. These can be turned blue by watering the surrounding soil with a solution of aluminium sulphate at a concentration of 1 ounce (28 grammes) in 4 gallons (18 litres) of water, or with a proprietary blueing powder. This is not very satisfactory, however, if the soil is strongly alkaline—in that case it is better to grow varieties that are naturally red or pink, whatever the acidity of the soil. All flower in late summer.

Hortensias

'Altona'—very large heads of blue flowers; looks better in a tub than in the open garden.
'Amethyst' — late-flowering; late summer/early autumn; violet-blue flowers with serrated petals.
'Ami Pasquier' is one of the earliest to flower; crimson in alkaline soil and purple in acid; relatively low-growing, about 3 feet (a metre) high.
'Gloire de Vendome' — crimson, dwarf-growing, late-flowering.
'Goliath'—tall-growing; small heads but large individual flowers of deep pink or blue-mauve; very good near sea.

'Hamburg'—deep blue in acid soil, bright pink in alkaline or neutral, very large flowers that darken to red in autumn.
'Joseph Banks'—vigorous and particularly good near sea. The flowers open cream then turn blue or pink.
'Madame Mouillière' has white, serrated flowers and flowers early. Probably the best white variety.
'Maréchal Foch' is deep blue in acid soil, rich pink in alkaline; very free-flowering.
'Vibraye' is bright blue on an acid soil and tall-growing. It has the great advantage of flowering from side-shoots even though the terminal bud has been frosted.
'Vulcain'—low-growing, only about 1 foot (30 cm) high. Deep blue or purple on acid soil, crimson on alkaline.
'Westfalen' is similar to the last but slightly taller and with even more richly coloured flowers.

Lacecaps

'Bluewave' is a vigorous, sometimes rather coarse shrub with blue or pink fertile flowers surrounded by ray florets that are deep blue in acid soil and dingy pink in alkaline.
'Lanarth White' is compact, only about 2 feet (60 cm) tall, with blue or pink fertile flowers surrounded by white ray florets.
'Lilacina' has blue or pink ray florets and leaves with a distinctive brown line round the edge.

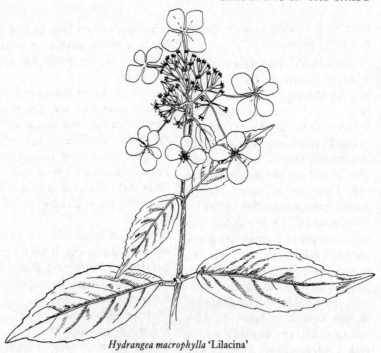

Hydrangea macrophylla 'Lilacina'

'Mariesii' is a Japanese variety with slightly rounded flower-heads, blue or pink according to soil.

'Tricolor' is probably a sport of the last variety; it has pink or pale blue flowers and leaves variegated with green, grey and yellow.

'Whitewave' is similar to 'Bluewave' but not so large and with white sterile flowers.

H. paniculata is a fairly large and floppy shrub with big, creamy-white panicles of flowers that turn pink as they age, in late summer/early autumn. It comes from China and Japan. 'Grandiflora' has extra-large panicles—so big that they make the plant look top-heavy. The pink tinge on fading is more pronounced.

'Praecox' flowers in July and has smaller panicles.

H. quercifolia is a native of the south-east United States. It has striking, large, lobed leaves that turn red in autumn, and white flowers often rather sparingly produced.

H. radiata is another American species, growing about 5 feet (1·5 metres) tall, with an upright habit. The leaves are white underneath and the creamy-white, scented flowers open in summer.

H. serrata is one of the most suitable species for the small garden as it is rarely taller than 3 feet (a metre). It is native to Japan and Korea. There are a number of cultivars: 'Bluebird' is small but vigorous, with blue fertile flowers surrounded by ray florets that are reddish-purple on alkaline soils and sea-blue on acid ones. 'Grayswood' is a lovely plant with pink fertile flowers and white ray florets that turn pink and finally crimson with age. These remain on the plant from late summer until late autumn or early winter.

KERRIA

K. japonica in the wild form is a very graceful shrub, usually about 4 feet (1·2 metres) tall, with green, arching branches covered with yellow flowers reminiscent of buttercups in late spring. It is better in shade as the flowers last longer. Unfortunately it is most often grown in the form 'Pleniflora' which is much less attractive. The flowers are double and rather muddled and the growth is much more erect and vigorous; if

Kerria japonica 'Golden Guinea'

this form is grown, it is best against a wall.

'Variegata' is an attractive form with leaves variegated with white and single flowers.

LINDERA

L. obtusiloba is a large, spreading shrub or a small tree with big, three-veined leaves, sometimes three-lobed at the tips, that turn bright yellow with pink tints in autumn—this is why it is grown. It does not grow on lime and likes woodland conditions; it may be damaged by frost in a hard winter. It comes from Japan, China and Korea.

LONICERA
See also p. 53.

L. tatarica comes from Russia and Turkestan and is very hardy; it grows well in sun or shade. It is a twiggy bush 6–8 feet (2–2·4 metres) high with small pink flowers in early summer followed by red berries. 'Alba' has white flowers and 'Arnold's Red' has deep pink flowers and larger berries.

MAGNOLIA
See also pp. 27 and 32.

M. liliiflora is a spreading shrub about 10–12 feet (3–3·6 metres) tall, with broad, glossy leaves. It has upright, tulip-shaped flowers, purplish outside and white inside, opening from late spring to early summer. It comes from central China, and dislikes chalk. 'Nigra' is a more compact plant with slightly larger flowers, deep purple outside and white marked with purple inside. This is the plant often called *M.* × *soulangeana* 'Nigra'.

Magnolia × *soulangeana* 'Nigra'

M. × *soulangeana* (*M. denudata* × *M. liliiflora*) is the most widely planted of all Magnolias, usually forming a large spreading shrub but sometimes quite a sizeable tree. It flowers reliably from an early age, with large, erect, tulip-shaped flowers in late spring, before the leaves appear— occasionally it is caught by late frosts. It is tolerant of atmospheric pollution and does well in towns and can stand some lime, but will not grow on chalk. Typically, the flowers are white flushed with purple, but there are many named clones.

'Alba Superba' is a lovely form, with pure white flowers.

'Alexandrina' grows strongly and flowers freely, with purple-flushed blooms.

'Brozzoni' has very large flowers with slight purple staining at the base that look like enormous candles.

'Lennei' is a vigorous form with flowers purple on the outside.

'Rustica Rubra' has reddish-pink flowers.

M. stellata is a hardy, slow-growing, spreading shrub, usually under 10 feet (3 metres), although I have seen it, when drawn up, form a gaunt tree of 20 feet (6 metres) or more. It has white, scented, starry flowers, produced in spring before the leaves. This is an attractive species and one of the best for general garden planting. 'Rosea' and 'Rubra' have pink flowers, the latter being deeper in colour. 'Water Lily' has larger flowers with more petals than those of the typical variety. If this species grows too large for its position, it can be spur-pruned immediately after flowering to keep it more compact.

Magnolia stellata

M. × *proctoriana* (*stellata* × *salicifol-ia*) is a fast-growing shrub with white flowers that open slightly earlier than those of either parent.

MENZIESIA

These are pretty, Ericaceous shrubs that are surprisingly seldom grown. They like lime-free soil and a sheltered position.

M. ciliicalyx, from Japan, grows slowly to about 3 feet (a metre) tall, with pendant, urn-shaped flowers in late spring and furry leaves. The flowers are usually dusky pink or soft purple but can be cream. Var. *pupurea* has larger, purple-pink flowers.

M. ferruginea is an American species slightly taller than the last with pale pink flowers.

M. pilosa is another American species, but from the east side instead of the west, with hanging clusters of pale yellow flowers, also in late spring.

POTENTILLA

The shrubby potentillas grow in any soil, in sun or partial shade. They flower more freely in the sun, but some varieties in particular need shade otherwise the colour of their flowers fades quickly. They are useful in having a very long flowering period, from early summer until late autumn.

P. arbuscula, from the Himalayas, is a small, hardy shrub with compound leaves with five leaflets and bright yellow flowers about an inch (2·5 cm) across, like small roses, from midsummer on. The form 'Beesii' has silvery foliage.

Potentilla arbuscula

P. fruticosa is a bush that can grow to 4 or 5 feet (about 1·5 metres) high. It is a very variable species, found in Europe, Asia and America. Typically, it has yellow flowers, but many cultivars are available.

'Beanii' has white flowers.

'Buttercup' has deep yellow flowers and is more compact than the typical form.

'Farrer's White' is also smallish, with white flowers.

'Katherine Dykes' is a vigorous form, up to 6 feet (2 metres) tall, with pale yellow flowers.

'Klondyke' is dwarf, with bright yellow flowers.

'Primrose Beauty'—grey-green leaves and pale yellow flowers.

'Sunset'—reddish-orange flowers.

'Tangerine'—orange-yellow flowers, spreading habit. Both these forms are better in shade.

'Vilmoriniana' is tall, up to 6 feet (2 metres), and upright in habit, with silvery leaves and creamy-white flowers.

Var. *mandschurica* is dwarf and spreading with grey-green leaves and white flowers.

'Elizabeth' is a cross between *P. arbuscula* and *P. fruticosa mandschurica* that forms a compact bush about 3 feet (a metre) high and as much across, with bright yellow flowers.

'Red Ace', the new cultivar of *P. fruticosa* that received a lot of publicity a while ago, with flame-red flowers, yellow on the reverse, seems to do better in a sunny position.

RHODODENDRON
See also pp. 27 and 60.

Many of the rhododendrons of the Azalea series are deciduous shrubs. There are some beautiful species that are not often grown and several groups of hybrids. As the latter are easily obtainable and there are so many of them, I shall not attempt to list individual varieties but just mention some of the groups available and their distinguishing characteristics. It is generally considered that azaleas are slightly easier to grow than other rhododendrons as they appear to be more tolerant of exposure and, in many cases, dryness. Also, while they do not grow in alkaline soil, they tend to do better than most rhododendrons in a soil approaching neutrality. However, they are seen at their best in light woodland, planted in drifts if space allows. In most species and varieties, the leaves colour well in autumn.

R. albrechtii is a lovely plant with wide-open, deep pink flowers in spring before the leaves appear. The young leaves are bronze when they first unfold and turn reddish-brown in autumn. It grows 6–10 feet (2–3 metres) tall, but is open in habit and not bulky-looking.

R. atlanticum is an American species growing to only about 3 feet (a metre); it spreads by stolons. It has clusters of white or pale pink scented flowers in late spring/early summer and in autumn the leaves turn brilliant scarlet.

R. calendulaceum, from eastern North America, is particularly hardy. It is an ancestor of many hybrid azaleas and has flowers that may be yellow, orange, pink or red, opening in early summer. The leaves turn red and yellow in autumn. It can grow to about 15 feet (4 metres) tall.

R. luteum is the common Pontic Azalea, but is a plant I like very much and would not wish to be without. The flowers are long-tubed, sticky and bright yellow with a heavy, honeysuckle perfume, and open in late spring/early summer just before the leaves unfold. It makes an open shrub up to 10 or 12 feet (around 3 metres) and seems to be very long-lived.

R. occidentale, another American species, is the chief parent of the Occidentale hybrids. It is large and vigorous, with sweetly scented, pink yellow-eyed flowers in mid-summer and very good autumn colour.

R. schlippenbachii comes from Korea

and Manchuria; it is very hardy but the leaves come out early, in spring, and so the first flush of growth is quite often frosted. It is an extremely beautiful plant that makes an open bush 12–15 feet (3·6–4 metres) tall, with large, shell-pink flowers appearing in late spring with the young leaves. These are bronze, and colour well again in autumn.

R. viscosum, from eastern North America, is known there as the Swamp Honeysuckle. It is useful in flowering late for an azalea, after mid-summer. The long-tubed flowers are white or pink, heavily perfumed, in large clusters.

Mollis hybrids

These are hardy, grow 5 to 6 feet (around 1·5 metres) tall, and flower in late spring/early summer just before the leaves appear. There is a wide colour range—cream, yellow, orange, salmon, pink and red—but they are rarely scented. There are probably hundreds of varieties available.

Ghent hybrids

These are even hardier than the last and usually flower a couple of weeks later. The colours are less vivid and the flowers are smaller than those of the Mollis hybrids, but the flowers are elegantly shaped with long tubes and pointed petals and have a heavy, sweet scent. There are a few double varieties such as 'Narcissiflorum'.

They and the Mollises were mostly bred in the last century.

Rustica Flore Pleno hybrids

These are all double, white, pink or yellow, and were developed in Belgium towards the end of the last century. They are less easily obtained than the last groups, but 'Norma' (pink tinged with apricot) and 'Phidias' (pink buds opening to cream flowers) are sometimes offered.

Occidentale hybrids

This group was developed early this century by crossing the Mollis hybrids with *R. occidentale*. The sweetly scented flowers are usually pink or white, with an orange flare, and open a week or two later than the Ghents. They grow 6–8 feet (about 2 metres) high.

Knap Hill and Exbury hybrids

These have been bred and selected from all the previous groups. The flowers are large, long-tubed but opening wide, in very large clusters. Many are scented, and they are found in every colour that deciduous azaleas come in—white, cream, yellow, salmon, orange, pink and red. Again, a vast selection is available.

RHODOTYPOS

R. scandens, the Jet Bead plant, is related to *Kerria japonica* and is very much like it. It has similar long, arching green stems but the flowers are white, about 2 inches (5 cm) across, opening in late spring/early summer, and are followed by round black fruits which give the plant its popular name. It grows in any situation and can tolerate dense shade.

RIBES

The currants. Most have gooseberry-like leaves and often they have hairy stems.

R. alpinum has greenish-yellow flowers followed by red berries. It is smallish and dense in habit and tolerates heavy shade. 'Aureum' has yellow leaves when young.

R. sanguineum, the Flowering Currant, is very well known. Although it comes from the west coast of North America, it is very hardy and grows in sun or shade. It has drooping racemes of pink flowers in spring with a peculiar smell that some people find quite pleasant and others think is like tomcats. These are followed by blue-purple berries. Many varieties are available, including 'Album' with white flowers and 'King Edward VII' with red flowers. 'Brocklebankii' is an attractive cultivar with golden leaves that must have shade.

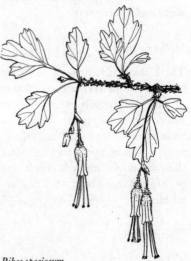

Ribes speciosum

Ribes sanguineum

R. speciosum is the most attractive of the currants, with glossy leaves that may be semi-evergreen and hanging, narrow red flowers rather like a Fuchsia's. In Britain, it is best against a sunny wall but in hot climates it needs partial shade.

RUBUS
See also p. 72.

R. cockburnianus has attractive ferny leaves and pinkish-purple flowers, but is grown mainly for its striking white stems. Old stems should be cut back to ground level every year after flowering, or the effect of the new growth will be lost. It comes from China.

R. deliciosus is a shrub about 5 feet (1·5 cm) tall, with arching branches and lobed leaves. The flowers are white with gold stamens, about 2 inches (5 cm) across, open in early summer. It comes from the Rocky Mountains.

R. trilobus is a Mexican native, similar to the last but with larger leaves and thornless stems. It flowers from late spring into summer.

Rubus 'Tridel'

'Tridel' is a vigorous and attractive hybrid between these two species with thornless shoots about 10 feet (3 metres) long, and 2-inch (5-cm)

white flowers with serrated petals and gold stamens all along the branches in early summer. 'Benenden' is a particularly good form. This and its parents would not do well in heavy shade.

R. × *fraseri* is a suckering shrub with large pink flowers from mid- to late summer that will grow under trees.

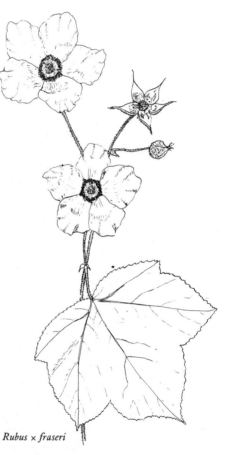

Rubus × *fraseri*

R. odoratus also spreads by suckers. It grows about 8 feet (2·4 metres) tall and has scented, purple-pink flowers

from mid-summer to early autumn
followed by edible red fruit. The
leaves are lobed and furry.

R. spectabilis has bright pink flowers
in spring, followed by edible orange
fruit. It is suckering and grows 4 or 5
feet (about 1·5 metres) tall. It and the
last species both grow under trees.

R. thibetanus is a Chinese species with
blue-white stems up to 6 feet (2
metres) long and downy, pinnate
grey-green leaves with a ferny effect.
Old flowering stems should be cut
back hard, as with *R. cockburnianus*.

SAMBUCUS

The Elders are grown more for
foliage than flower. All have pinnate
leaves, and if so desired, they can be
pruned in late autumn or early
spring.

S. callicarpa, from eastern North
America, is a shrub growing to
15 feet (4 metres) or so that will
tolerate deep shade. It has round
heads of white flowers in summer,
followed by red berries that are not
edible.

S. nigra, the Common Elder, forms
a large shrub or small tree. It is often
considered more or less a weed, but
there are several attractive cultivars.
'Albovariegata' has leaves bordered
with white; 'Aurea', the Golden
Elder, has golden-yellow leaves that
keep their colour throughout the
season. 'Laciniata', the Fern-leafed
Elder, has very finely-cut leaves.

S. racemosa, the Red-berried Elder,

has conical heads of white flowers
followed by red berries. Although not
a British native (it comes from other
parts of Europe and west Asia) it has
become naturalised in some places,
particularly in Scotland. The variety
'Plumosa Aurea' is one of the best of
all golden-leaved shrubs with richly
coloured, deeply-cut leaves.

STACHYURUS

Shrubs that flower on the bare wood
in spring and grow in sun or partial
shade. The habit is not particularly
attractive, but this could be con-
cealed by a low evergreen in front.
They do well in Australia, and should
be much more widely grown in
Britain.

S. chinensis is a large, spreading
shrub with long racemes of pale
yellow flowers in mid-spring. It is
native to China. 'Magpie' is a form
with white-edged leaves.

Stachyurus praecox

S. praecox grows 6–8 feet (2–2·4
metres) tall, and has drooping
racemes of primrose-yellow, cup-
shaped flowers opening in mid-

spring that look from a distance like strings of berries. It comes from Japan, and will grow in quite a heavily shaded situation.

STAPHYLEA

The Bladder-nuts grow as large shrubs or small trees. They are hardy and accommodating, growing in sun or partial shade. In flower, the general effect is rather like that of a white cherry, but in close-up it can be seen that the flowers have five spreading white sepals and five petals standing straight out like a tube. I cannot think why they are not more widely grown.

S. colchica grows 10 to 15 feet (3–4 metres) high, and has 6-inch (15-cm) panicles of white flowers in late spring/early summer. The leaves have three to five narrow leaflets, toothed so finely that they look fringed. 'Coulombieri' is more vigorous, with larger leaves.

Staphylea colchica

S. × elegans is a hybrid between the last species and the very similar *S. pinnata*. It has larger hanging flower clusters than the last, and the leaves usually have five leaflets. 'Hessei' has flowers flushed with red.

STEPHANANDRA

Shrubs related to Spiraea that grow in any soil, in sun or partial shade.

S. incisa, from Japan, has lobed leaves and panicles of white flowers in mid-summer. It usually grows 5 or 6 feet (about 1·5 metres) tall.

S. tanakae, also from Japan, is similar to the last but flowers and leaves are both slightly larger.

SYMPHORICARPOS

These plants are useful in that they grow in any soil and under trees, and birds do not eat their berries—the reason for their being grown.

S. albus, Snowberry, is a small, suckering shrub from east North America with white berries.

S. × doorenbosii is a hybrid originating in Holland that grows about 5 feet (1·5 metres) tall and has pink-tinged, white berries. There are several named clones; one of the best is 'Mother of Pearl' which has large fruit, very freely borne.

S. rivularis, from west North America, is another shrub called Snowberry; this is the one most often seen in Britain, with large, white berries following small, pink flowers. It is a

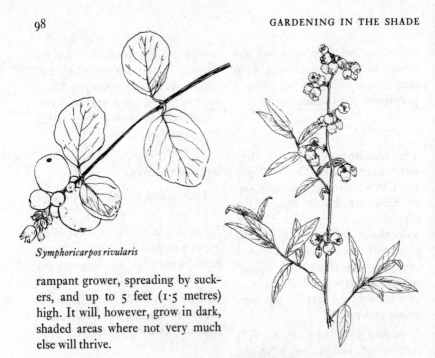

Symphoricarpos rivularis

rampant grower, spreading by suckers, and up to 5 feet (1·5 metres)
high. It will, however, grow in dark,
shaded areas where not very much
else will thrive.

VACCINIUM

A large genus related to heather
which, while not showy, has a quiet
charm; many species have edible
fruit. They must have an acid soil
and some species will grow in sun or
partial shade, although others need
full exposure.

V. angustifolium, Low-bush Blueberry, is a shrub growing to 2 or 3
feet (up to a metre), with clusters of
greenish-white, bell-shaped flowers
in spring and leaves that are a lovely
fresh green when young and colour
well in autumn. It has blue-black
edible berries that are rather less
freely produced in shade—it is
grown for its fruit in North America.
Var. *laevifolium*, once known as *V.
pensylvanicum*, has larger leaves.

Vaccinium angustifolium var. *laevifolium*

V. corymbosum, High-bush Blueberry or Swamp Blueberry, grows to
4 or 5 feet (about 1·5 metres). It has
bright green leaves, turning red in
autumn, and pink or white urn-
shaped flowers in late spring/early
summer followed by edible blue-
black berries. It comes from eastern
North America and is widely grown
there for fruit.

VIBURNUM
See also p. 74.

V. × bodnantense (*V. farreri* × *V.
grandiflorum*) flowers from autumn
to early spring, with round heads of
white, pink-flushed flowers that can
resist a few degrees of frost. It is a
strong-growing plant, that can reach

Viburnum × bodnantense

8 feet (2·4 metres) or so. There are a number of clones; two of the best are 'Dawn' and 'Deben', both with pink buds opening to white flowers.

V. × carlcephalum (*carlesii × macro-cephalum*) also grows to about 8 feet (2·4 metres), although it is compact rather than straggling, and has clusters of white flowers opening from pink buds in late spring/early summer. The leaves often colour well in autumn.

V. carlesii, from Korea, has round heads of heavily-perfumed white flowers opening from pink buds in late spring. It is rather prone to aphid attack, although less so when grown in some shade, and if this is noticed the plant should be sprayed with a systemic insecticide such as 'Rogor'. There are several clones, including 'Aurora' and 'Diana', both with red buds opening to pink flowers, and 'Charis', with deep pink buds.

V. farreri, once called *V. fragrans*, has pink buds opening to white scented flowers in clusters on the bare twigs throughout the winter. It comes from northern China, and can reach 10 or 12 feet (3–3·6 metres). The toothed leaves are bronze when young. Var. *candidissimum* has pure white flowers and green new growth. 'Nanum' is dwarf and compact in habit, but is less free-flowering than the typical form.

V. foetens, from Korea and the Himalayas, has round heads of scented white flowers on stout stems from late winter to spring. The clusters open from fat, sticky buds like miniature horse chestnuts. It grows to 6 or 8 feet (2–2·4 metres) with a spreading habit and must have some shade. I used to wonder why the unflattering name of *foetens* (stinking) was applied to this sweetly scented plant, but I find it refers to the bark, which smells nasty when damaged. This species now includes the plant previously known as *V. grandiflorum*.

V. furcatum is very different in appearance from those just mentioned. It has flat heads of white flowers, surrounded by some large, sterile ray florets, in late spring/early summer. The leaves are almost round and turn maroon-crimson in autumn. It is quite a large shrub, native to Japan and Korea, and dislikes lime.

V. × juddii is a bushy plant growing 4 or 5 feet (about 1·5 metres) tall with clusters of pinkish flowers in late spring. It is more compact than *V. carlesii*, which it resembles, and is less likely to be attacked by aphids.

V. plicatum is a spreading shrub about 8 feet (2·4 metres) high with heads of white, sterile flowers in early summer borne along the length of each branch. This seems to be a form long cultivated in China and Japan. 'Grandiflorum' has larger flowering heads and pink-tinged florets. Var. *tomentosum* is one of the best of all garden shrubs, with almost horizontal branches giving a tiered effect. It has flat heads of fertile flowers surrounded by white sterile florets (rather like a lace-cap hydrangea) in double rows along the tops of the branches in early summer. The leaves usually colour well in autumn. The plant's only drawback is that it needs plenty of space to show up the beauty of its shape. There are some particularly good selected clones, such as 'Lanarth' and 'Mariesii'— probably the most effective of all, with completely horizontal branches and larger florets than the typical form. 'Rowallane' is less vigorous than these last two cultivars and so is more suitable for a small garden, although it has equal architectural effect.

Viburnum plicatum

WEIGELA

These are very easily grown and hardy shrubs that do well in sun or part shade and are tolerant of atmospheric pollution. They have tubular flowers, and should be cut back each year after flowering.

W. florida is the most widely grown species, with pink flowers in early summer. It comes from Japan, Korea and northern China. 'Variegata' is a very pretty cultivar with clear pink flowers and leaves bordered with white. It grows about 4 feet (1·2 metres) tall—the typical form tends to be larger.

Many of the plants grown in gardens are hybrids or cultivars of the last species.

'Abel Carriere' has large, bright pink flowers from darker buds.

'Bristol Ruby' has red flowers.

'Eva Rathke' has deep wine-crimson flowers over a long period and is fairly compact in habit.

'Looymansii Aurea' has golden foliage and pink flowers and needs some shade.

XANTHORRHIZA

X. simplicissima, Yellow-root, is a suckering shrub from the eastern United States that will tolerate dense shade. It forms large clumps about 3 feet (a metre) high, with toothed, pinnate leaves that turn bronze in autumn, and clusters of small purple flowers in early spring. It dislikes chalk and is best in a moist situation.

ZENOBIA

Z. pulverulenta is a beautiful small shrub, sometimes semi-evergreen, with hanging clusters of creamy, bell-shaped flowers in summer. It likes a moist soil with plenty of humus, lime-free and some shade – this last being, as usual, more important when grown in hot climates like Australia's. It comes from the eastern United States.

7

Herbaceous Plants

ACTAEA

The Baneberries are naturally woodland plants; they stand dense shade
as long as it is not too dry.

A. alba, White Baneberry, has
racemes of white flowers in spring
and early summer, followed by
white berries.

A. rubra, Red Baneberry, has ferny
leaves and red berries.

A. spicata has black berries.

AJUGA

Good ground-cover plants, they are
low-growing and spreading and
retain their leaves all the year round.

A. pyramidalis has glossy leaves and
spikes of vivid blue flowers about 6
inches (15 cm) high in late spring.

A. reptans, Bugle, spreads rapidly
and can become rampant. There are
several clones with coloured foliage
which do not retain that colour in
dense shade. All have blue flowers in
late spring/early summer, in spikes
about 4 inches (10 cm) high.
'Burgundy Glow' has pink and
purple leaves, many edged with
cream.
'Multicolor' has bronze leaves marked with pink and cream.
'Purpurea' has rich purple leaves.
'Variegata' has leaves variegated with
creamy white.

Ajuga reptans 'Burgundy Glow'

ALCHEMILLA

A. mollis, Lady's Mantle, has downy,
rounded leaves with toothed edges
and feathery sprays of yellow-green
flowers throughout the summer.

ALSTROEMERIA

Peruvian Lily.

A. aurantiaca has orange-yellow lily-
like flowers over a long period in
summer on 3-foot (1-metre) stems.
It has fleshy roots and spreads
rapidly.
'Ligtu Hybrids' have a wide colour
range—yellow, orange, pink and red.

ANEMONE

An important genus of shade-loving plants that are mostly woodland species in the wild. They have no petals; the sepals are the colourful part.

A. apennina has divided leaves and vivid blue flowers with many sepals in spring. It grows only 6 or 8 inches (15–20 cm) tall. Pink, mauve and white forms are available.

A. blanda is very similar to the last, but slightly smaller although the flowers are if anything larger, and earlier—appearing in early spring.

Anemone blanda

A. narcissiflora, the Apple-blossom Anemone, has hairy, ferny leaves and white flowers tinged with pink in summer. It is 8–12 inches (20–30 cm) high.

A.×hybrida. The Japanese Anemones are still sometimes listed as *A. japonica* or *A. hupehensis*. They are tall, sometimes as much as 3 or 4 feet (about a metre) and flower in late summer/early autumn, the colours being white or various shades of pink or mauve. They thrive in quite heavy shade. Many cultivars are available, including 'Louise Uhink'—white, 'Prince Henry' (also known as 'Profusion')—deep pink, and 'Queen Charlotte'—pale pink.

A. nemorosa. The Wood Anemone is well worth a place in a garden; it looks beautiful naturalised under trees. It has starry white flowers tinged with pink in spring and divided leaves. Some forms are pale blue or mauve.

A. vitifolia is similar to *A.×hybrida*, but flowers earlier, in late summer. The flowers are pink and very freely produced. It has vine-like leaves as the name suggests.

ANEMONELLA

A. thalictroides, the Rue Anemone, is a delicate-looking woodland plant, rather like the Wood Anemone, with rue-like foliage and white or pale pink flowers in spring.

ANEMONOPSIS

A. macrophylla is a Japanese woodland species with divided leaves and hanging purple and white flowers on stalks 2 feet (60 cm) long in late summer/early autumn.

AQUILEGIA

Most of the Columbines will grow in light shade. There are quite a number of species, but the most spectacular plants are the Long-spurred Hybrids, which come in almost every colour and combination of colours.

ARISAEMA

These plants are related to the Arum Lily and have a similar type of flower. They do best in a peaty soil, with plenty of moisture but good drainage.

A. candidissimum has a white, hooded spathe tinged with pink, and one trifoliate leaf per plant.

A. ringens has green or purple spathes.

A. triphyllum is an American species that will grow in quite dense shade, and may become naturalised. It has hooded green spathes striped with white and brown, about 12 inches (30 cm) high.

ARISARUM

A. proboscideum, the Mouse Tail, or Mouse Plant, grows in sun or shade but does better in the latter, and will tolerate quite heavy shade. It is an amusing if not a showy plant, again related to the Arums, with the spathe prolonged into a long, narrow structure which looks like a mouse's tail protruding from the glossy leaves. It flowers in spring and is 6–8 inches (15–20 cm) high.

ARTEMESIA

A. lactiflora. Most of this genus, with its grey-green, aromatic leaves, are sun-lovers, but this species will grow in partial shade. It has greenish-white flowers.

ARUM

A. italicum 'Pictum' has green arrow-shaped leaves with a network of white markings that appear in winter and remain fresh until summer. It has green, arum-like flowers followed by spikes of red berries. It is better in a fairly moist position.

A. maculatum, Lords and Ladies or Cuckoo Pint, is a well-known British native. The arrow-shaped leaves are sometimes all green and sometimes spotted with blackish brown. It has greenish-white spathes in spring followed by spikes of bright red berries and is worth a place in a woodland garden or in the shade of a hedge.

ARUNCUS

A. sylvester, Goat's Beard, is a striking plant for a shaded position, with ferny leaves and feathery plumes of creamy-white flowers in summer, 4–6 feet (1·2–2 metres) tall. It needs plenty of moisture.

ASARUM

Known for some reason as the Wild Gingers. All are shade-lovers and are normally evergreen, except *A. cana-*

dense, although they may die back in an exceptionally cold winter.

A. europaeum, Asarabacca or European Wild Ginger, is a creeping plant with round, glossy evergreen leaves about 3 inches (7 cm) across that form a dense carpet if the soil is not too dry. The flowers in this and all the other species are inconspicuous —brownish and often hidden by the leaves. It is used as a ground cover in Britain and America.

A. arifolia has sagittate leaves with silvery mottling in summer, turning purplish in winter.

A. canadense has attractive hairy leaves, but is less useful as it is deciduous.

A. caudatum is found in moist woods on the west coast of America. The leaves are heart-shaped or kidney-shaped, less glossy than those of *A. europaeum* and sometimes reddish below.

A. shuttleworthii has longer and narrower leaves than the other species.

A. virginica (sometimes called *Hexastylis virginica*) is rather variable in foliage, but the leaves are often heart-shaped and marbled with silvery white, up to 3 inches (7 cm) long.

ASPERULA

A. odorata, Sweet Woodruff, is not at all showy but is a pleasant little plant with whorls of bright green leaves and heads of small, starry white flowers in late spring. The leaves smell of new-mown hay when dried. It spreads quite rapidly but is not invasive.

ASTILBE

Still commonly known as 'Spiraea', although botanically that name is now confined to shrubby species. There are many hybrids available in different colours—red, pink and white—all with pretty, ferny leaves, often bronze in spring. As well as partial shade, they like a moist position; they do well at the edge of a pond.

A. chinensis 'Pumila' is a dwarf species only about 1 foot (30 cm) high with sprays of pink flowers in late summer/early autumn.

BEGONIA

In Britain, begonias are usually grown in full sun but in America and Australia, both the tuberous begonias and the small-flowered bedding variety known as *B. semperflorens* are widely grown as shade plants where, of course, they provide a mass of vivid colour. So many forms are available that there is no point in listing them, as they can be found in any catalogue.

BERGENIA

These are splendid, evergreen ground-cover plants that grow in sun or shade. They have large, round, leathery leaves (I have heard the plant called 'Elephant's Ears') that often turn bronze or reddish in winter. They look very handsome in town gardens growing beside paving. They have dense heads of red, pink or white flowers on stems 1–1½ feet (30–45 cm) long in spring—it is important to obtain a good form as some are much less impressive than others. The following are among the best:

'Abendglut' ('Evening Glow')—deep magenta-purple flowers; leaves purple in winter.

'Ballawley'—deep red flowers, but leaves can be lost in a cold winter.

B. cordifolia var. *pupurea* is one of the finest of all for foliage, with leaves that turn rich purple in autumn and winter, and purple-red flowers.

B. crassifolia has spoon-shaped leaves (curved side up) that are red-bronze in winter, and pink flowers in spring. 'Silberlicht'—white flowers tinged with pink. 'Sunningdale'—pink flowers; leaves dark red in winter, purple on the reverse side.

BLETIA (BLETILLA)

B. hyacinthina is a hardy orchid that likes partial shade. It has long, light green leaves with prominent parallel veins and sprays of red-purple flowers in summer, about 1 foot (30 cm) tall.

BOYKINIA

These are woodland plants, related to *Saxifrage*.

B. aconitifolia has heads of creamy-white flowers in summer, about 2½ feet (75 cm) tall, and pleasant foliage.

B. occidentalis is a North American species, with lobed, serrated reddish leaves and panicles of white flowers in summer.

B. tellimoides is a larger plant. It has rounded, lobed and serrated leaves about 6 inches (15 cm) across and racemes of white flowers about 2 feet (60 cm) tall, in summer.

BRUNNERA

B. macrophylla has sprays of bright blue flowers, like a giant forget-me-not, from spring to mid-summer. The dark green, hairy, heart-shaped leaves grow larger throughout the summer. It is a fine ground-cover plant both in woodland and in a town garden. 'Variegata' is a handsome form whose leaves are variegated with creamy yellow.

CAMPANULA

This is a very large genus, including many rock-garden species. Some of these are shade-tolerant, and in hotter climates require shade. The taller, herbaceous species grow in sun or shade.

C. alariifolia has hairy, heart-shaped grey-green leaves and arching stems about 18 inches (45 cm) high with hanging creamy white bell-shaped flowers in summer.

C. glomerata has heads of deep violet-purple flowers in summer, again about 18 inches (45 cm) tall. There are a number of cultivars, including some with white flowers.

C. lactiflora has violet-blue bells borne on leafy stems, 5 or 6 feet (about 1·5 metres) tall. There is a pink variety.

Of the dwarf species, *C. carpatica* and *C. portenschlagiana* are particularly shade-tolerant. The former has widely cup-shaped erect flowers of blue or white, while the latter has hanging blue-purple bells in summer. It does well against a shaded wall—it can become rampant if given too much room.

CARDAMINE

C. asarifolia, a relative of the native Lady's Smock, has racemes of four-petalled white flowers in early summer. The heart-shaped leaves are like those of Asarum.

C. trifolia has leaves with three round leaflets and white flowers in late spring/early summer of 6-inch (15-cm) stems. Both of these thrive in quite deep shade.

CARDIOCRINUM

C. giganteum, once known as *Lilium giganteum*, is a magnificent woodland species that may be as much as 10 feet (3 metres) tall, with heads of narrowly trumpet-shaped white flowers, 6 inches (15 cm) long in summer. The leaves are heart-shaped and dark, glossy green. The main bulb dies after flowering but some offsets remain.

CAULOPHYLLUM

C. thalictroides, Blue Cohosh, from east North America, has yellowish flowers tinged with purple in late spring followed by blue fruit, and one large, divided leaf. It grows about 2 feet (60 cm) tall. *C. robustum* is a Japanese species that is very similar.

CHELONE

C. obliqua, Turtle Flower, has pink flowers on stalks 2–3 feet (upto a metre) tall from mid-summer till early autumn. It forms large clumps in a moist, rich soil.

CHIASTOPHYLLUM

C. oppositifolium has round, succulent leaves and drooping racemes of small yellow flowers. It grows only about 4 inches (10 cm) high.

CHIMAPHILA

C. maculata has roundish, evergreen leaves with white veining and white flowers in summer, only about 5 inches (12 cm) high. It needs acid soil, but will tolerate fairly dry conditions.

C. umbellata has toothed leaves in whorls of three and clusters of pink and white flowers. Neither of these species is very vigorous or easily grown.

CHRYSOGONUM

C. virginianum, Golden Star, is an American native with yellow, starry

flowers borne over a long period—
from spring to late summer. It grows
about 6 inches (15 cm) high and has
evergreen or semi-evergreen foliage,
and does best in partial shade.

CIMICIFUGA

C. racemosa, Bugbane or Black
Snakeroot, is a fine plant for a shaded
border where the soil is fairly moist.
It has ferny leaves and 5-foot (1·5-
metre) branched racemes of white
flowers from mid-summer to early
autumn. *C. americana* is similar, but
smaller.

CLINTONIA

C. andrewsiana belongs to the Liliaceae. It has pinkish-purple bell-
shaped flowers on a 2-foot (60-cm)
stem followed by purple berries,
from a rosette of bright green leaves.

COLCHICUM

The autumn crocuses, as they are
often called, are not true crocuses.
The most obvious difference is in the
leaves, which are narrow and grassy
in Crocus and large and broad in
Colchicum. There are a number of
species and hybrids, some of which
are better with full sun.

C. speciosum, although it grows in
sun, also does well in shade—I have
seen it more or less naturalised in
light woodland. It has large, tulip-
like flowers in autumn, appearing
from the bare ground. Typically they
are mauve-pink, but they can be

reddish-purple or white. A number
of named clones are available. The
leaves are large and rather floppy and
appear in spring—these leaves make
the plant slightly difficult to place as
they take up a considerable amount
of room.

CONVALLARIA

C. majalis, the Lily-of-the-Valley, is
too well known to need much
description. The racemes of creamy-
white, heavily scented flowers open
in late spring/early summer and are
sometimes followed by quite decorative red berries. It spreads rapidly
by underground stems and grows in
dense shade and dry situations,
sometimes coming up in cracks
between paving stones. 'Fortin's
Giant' has larger flowers, opening
slightly later. There is a form with
variegated leaves which I have not
seen.

CORTUSA

C. matthiola is related to the Primrose and likes similar woodland
conditions. It has crinkled, hairy,
lobed leaves and umbels of hanging
red-purple flowers on stems 6–9
inches (15–22 cm) long in early
summer. 'Alba' is a white form.

CYCLAMEN

An important shade-loving genus.
They grow on acid, alkaline or
neutral soils and are best under
trees—even under ones which cast
dense shade, such as yews and ever-

green oaks. They do well in dry conditions, but can be grown in areas of high rainfall provided drainage is good. All have tubers which do not multiply, but many spread freely by seed. The florist's cyclamen can be grown in a shady position in Australia, but cannot be grown outside all the year round in Britain.

C. coum is a very variable species. The leaves may be plain green or splashed with silver; round or kidney-shaped; red or green underneath. The flowers are pink, red or white, and open from mid-winter to spring. Although it is hardy, the flowers and foliage may be damaged by frost and cold winds so it needs some shelter.

C. hederifolium is the species probably better known as *C. neapolitanum*. It is the easiest of all the species to grow and does well on any soil except heavy clay. One peculiarity is that the roots come from the *upper* surface of the tuber, and the tubers should be planted, near the surface, with these uppermost. They benefit from dressings of leaf-mould. The flowers are pink or sometimes white and open in late summer and autumn; they are followed immediately by the leaves which are usually beautifully marbled with white and are as decorative as the flowers. These last until about mid-summer. I have seen the leaves dark and limp with frost, but they soon revive. It is reputed not to like atmospheric pollution.

C. purpurascens (*C. europaeum*) flowers from mid-summer until late autumn. It is very free-flowering if conditions are right but it is not as easy to suit or as hardy as *C. hederifolium*. It seems to do best in beech or oak leaf-mould, and must have good drainage. It seems to have a preference for limestone areas. The leaves are evergreen and may be plain green or patterned with white. The flowers are pink, with a crimson patch at the base of each petal, and sweetly scented. The roots come from all surfaces of the tuber.

C. repandum has thin leaves that are easily damaged by hot sunlight, but it is also not suitable for a cold area. The leaves have a toothed margin and are marbled with white or silver and are usually red-purple below. The flowers are red, pink or white and open in late spring.

C. africanum, *C. cilicium* and *C. graecum* are autumn-flowering species whose leaves usually unfold at the same time as the flowers. The first is a large handsome species that needs a frame or alpine house in Britain and other temperate zones; the other two have been grown outside successfully in some gardens in these areas. All three do well in shade in Australia, particularly in the Melbourne area.

CYPRIPEDIUM

The Lady's Slipper Orchids.

C. calceolus is one of the rarest of British native plants, but is less rare elsewhere—it has a circum-polar distribution in the northern hemisphere. The flowers are large, on 12-inch (30-cm) stems, with the lip developed into a curious yellow pouch, and the other petals dark purple. Although it grows on limestone in the wild, this is not necessary in gardens.

C. pubescens is an American species with the lateral petals greenish rather than purple.

DEINANTHE

D. bifida, from Japan, likes a moist, shaded situation and, given that, spreads by creeping rhizomes. It has two-lobed leaves and round, waxy white flowers in late summer on 2-foot (60-cm) stems.

D. carulea has roundish, coarsely serrated leaves and hanging, cup-shaped blue-lilac flowers in late summer. It grows about 1 foot (30 cm) tall. Both species are very hardy.

DICENTRA

This genus includes a number of species, with attractive, ferny foliage and oddly-shaped, locket-like flowers.

D. cucullaria is only 5 or 6 inches (12–15 cm) tall and has creamy flowers with yellow tips.

D. eximia, Dutchman's Breeks, has deep pink, hanging flowers open over a long period in spring and early summer. It grows about 1 foot

(30 cm) tall. The dense clumps of feathery leaves make an effective ground cover, and it seems to do well under trees. Some cultivars are available with red or white flowers.

D. spectabilis, Bleeding Heart or Lady's Locket, is slightly larger and if anything more handsome, with broader leaf segments and pink and white flowers.

DIERAMA

D. pulcherrima, Fairy's Wand or Fairy's Fishing-rod, is a charming South African species that is not hardy in a cold district but dislikes hot, dry situations. It has iris-like leaves and long, wiry stems up to 5 feet (1·5 metres) tall, arching at the tips and bearing hanging, bell-shaped flowers that may be pink, mauve, purple or white. Several named clones are available. It is very pretty in a shaded border and, although tall, does not take up much room.

DIGITALIS

The Foxgloves. There are a number of species and hybrids, most of which are very suitable for a shaded garden.

D. ambigua (*grandiflora*) has spikes of deep yellow flowers about 2 feet (60 cm) tall and velvety foliage.

D. ferruginea has copper-yellow 'gloves' on stems 3–4 feet (around a metre) tall.

D. lutea—slender spikes of narrow, yellow flowers, 3–4 feet (around a metre) tall.

D. mertonensis—pink flowers, 2–3 feet (up to a metre) tall.

D. purpurea. The wild form has rose-purple flowers spotted inside, but there are also white forms and various cultivated strains with pink or apricot flowers. The flower-spikes are 2–4 feet (around a metre) tall and come from rosettes of grey-green furry leaves. They are biennials, not true perrenials, but seed profusely and become naturalised.

DIPHYLLEIA

D. cymosa, Umbrella Leaf, is an unusual-looking American woodland species that grows in quite dense shade. It has large leaves, about a foot (30 cm) across, deeply cleft into two. Heads of small white flowers in early summer are followed by purple-black fruit. *D. grayi* is a Japanese species that is rather similar.

DODECATHEON

The American Cowslips or Shooting Stars are related to Primula, but the petals are reflexed (as in Cyclamen) and the stamens protrude. They like woodland conditions.

D. meadia, the most widely grown species, has heads of pink or some-times white flowers on stalks 1–2 feet (30–60 cm) tall in early summer.

D. jeffreyi is usually slightly taller,

with many purple flowers on one stalk and large, light green leaves.

D. radicatum is smaller, to about a foot (30 cm), with glossy leaves and rosy-purple flowers.

ENDYMION

The bluebells are still sometimes listed under *Scilla*. Two species are grown in gardens; both are at their best in woodland although they will grow in a border, and naturalise freely. If the species are grown together, they hybridise readily.

E. hispanicus, the Spanish Bluebell, has larger, more wide-open bells and bigger spikes of flower than the native species, but it has very little scent. Typically, the flowers are sky blue, lighter than the wild bluebell, but many colour forms are available, including deep blue, pink and white.

E. non-scriptus is the wild bluebell. It also has pink and white forms.

EOMECON

E. chionanthum, Chinese Poppy, has white, poppy-like flowers with gold stamens in summer, about 1 foot (30 cm) tall. It has pale green heart-shaped leaves with scalloped edges.

EPIMEDIUM

These are graceful plants related to Berberis with wiry stems and leaf-stalks. Some species are evergreen, but with them it is better to cut the old leaves away in spring to make way for the young growth which is often flushed with red or bronze. They grow in dense shade and suppress pretty well all weeds. There are many species and hybrids, and the names are often confused. Most flower in late spring.

E. alpinum has pale green leaves, tinged with red, and small, reddish-purple flowers on thin stalks about 1 foot (30 cm) tall.

E. grandiflorum—leaves with a serrated edge, with white, pink or violet flowers.

E. pinnatum has bright green leaves and yellow flowers.

E. × rubrum has sprays of red and yellow flowers on 15-inch (38-cm) stalks.

E. × versicolor 'Sulphureum' has relatively large, pale yellow flowers. It is deciduous.

E. × youngianum has white flowers, about a foot (30 cm) tall. 'Niveum' is dwarfer, with leaves that are bronze in spring.

ERANTHIS

E. hyemalis, the Winter Aconite, is one of the earliest of the spring bulbs to flower. It has bright yellow, buttercup-like flowers with a bright green leafy bract forming a ruff immediately below. It is only 3 or 4 inches (7–10 cm) high and grows well under deciduous trees.

Eranthis hyemalis

ERINUS

E. alpinus is a very small, tufted alpine plant with pink flowers coming from rosettes of leaves in spring. It does well in cracks on a shady wall—it is short-lived but seeds itself freely. There is a white form, and 'Dr Hanele' has red flowers.

ERYTHRONIUM

Beautiful spring-flowering plants belonging to the Liliaceae that are best suited by a moist situation in semi-shade. When they are moved, the bulbs should not be allowed to dry out. There are a number of species, mostly American.

E. californicum has white flowers, several per stem, from spring to mid-summer, and leaves marbled with white. It grows usually about 1 foot (30 cm) tall.

E. dens-canis is a European species, again with marbled leaves, and pink flowers with reflexed petals borne on

6-inch (15-cm) stems. There are forms with white and purple flowers.

E. grandiflorum, the Glacier Lily, comes from west North America and has large, yellow flowers and un-mottled leaves.

E. hendersonii is a vigorous species, flowering in spring, with mottled leaves and clusters of mauve flowers marked with purple.

E. oregonum has 2-foot (60-cm) tall spikes of white flowers. 'White Beauty' is a very good and vigorous form that is thought to be a natural hybrid of this species.

E. revolutum, the Trout Lily, has mottled leaves and clusters of large pink or white flowers with markedly recurved petals in late spring.

E. tuolumnense is rather similar to *E. grandiflorum*, with yellow flowers and plain green leaves. It is a good garden plant and forms large clumps when conditions are to its liking. 'Pagoda' is a hybrid of this species that is slightly taller—18 inches (45 cm)—and has larger flowers.

EUPHORBIA

Many of the spurges are sun-lovers, but there are quite a number of species that require shade.

E. amygdaloides, the native Wood Spurge, tolerates dense shade. It grows 1–2 feet (30–60 cm) high and has yellow-green flowers and grey-green leaves, reddish when they are young.

E. cyparissias makes a pleasant ground cover, with narrow leaves and lime-green flowers, 9–12 inches (22–30 cm) high.

E. robbiae, Mrs Robb's Bonnet, has dark evergreen leaves and lime green flowers; it grows about 2 feet (60 cm) high. It is very similar to *E. amyg-daloides* and may, indeed, be the same species.

E. sikkimensis is a large species grow-ing to about 4 feet (1·2 metres). The shoots are red in spring and gradu-ally turn green; the yellow-green flowers are borne in late summer. It will not tolerate heavy shade.

FILIPENDULA

F. purpurea has large, divided leaves and tall heads of fluffy pink flowers up to 4 feet (1·2 metres) tall in summer.

F. ulmaria 'Aurea' is the golden-leaved form of 'Meadowsweet'. The vivid golden leaves scorch in hot sun; the flowers are insignificant—in fact they are better removed. It needs a rich, moist soil.

GALANTHUS

The Snowdrops.

G. nivalis is the common snowdrop, found wild in woods over a large part of Europe. This species tolerates quite heavy shade although it also grows in open situations provided the soil is sufficiently moist. The usual flowering time is the end of winter and early spring. There are many varieties and cultivars. Var. *flavescens* and var. *lutescens* have yellow markings instead of green on the petals. 'Atkinsii' is a vigorous and large-flowered variety.

G. elwesii is an altogether larger species than the last, with broad, glaucous green leaves and thick stems. It flowers in early and mid-spring.

G. plicatus is another larger species, with broad leaves recurved at the margins.

GALAX

G. aphylla is an American woodland plant, with round, glossy evergreen leaves sometimes tinged with red (good for flower arrangement). It has spikes of white flowers in early summer, 12–18 inches (30–45 cm) tall. It needs a peaty soil.

GENTIANA

Most gentians are plants of alpine meadows and like an open situation, but there are some that prefer shade.

G. asclepiadea, the Willow Gentian, is a woodland species from southern Europe and does well in a shaded border. It has willowy leaves and bright blue trumpet-shaped flowers along 2-foot (60-cm) stalks in late summer/early autumn.

G. lutea grows 3 or 4 feet (around a metre) tall and has yellow flowers.

GERANIUM

These should not be confused with the plants popularly called geraniums, which really belong to the genus *Pelargonium*. They are perfectly hardy and all have attractive lobed or divided foliage and smother weeds efficiently. Most grow in sun or shade, even under trees.

G. endressii has finely divided leaves and pink flowers from mid-summer to early autumn; it grows 12–18 inches (30–45 cm) high. 'Wargrave' has bright salmon pink flowers.

G. grandiflorum has violet-blue, veined flowers with a reddish eye in summer, and finely divided leaves that turn red in autumn. It forms clumps about 1 foot (30 cm) high and as much across.

G. ibericum has violet-purple flowers with darker veining from early to late summer.

'Johnson's Blue' has vivid violet-blue flowers from early to late summer.

G. macrorrhizum has lilac flowers from early to mid-summer and light green leaves, scented when crushed. There is a variegated form that does well in shade. This is one of the best ground-cover species.

G. nodosum has glossy leaves and lilac pink flowers over a long period; it does well even in dense shade.

G. phaeum, the Mourning Widow, has flowers that are a very dark maroon, almost black, with a white spot at the base of each petal. It flowers in early summer.

G. pratense makes large clumps 3 feet (a metre) tall and as much across. It has violet-blue flowers in summer. Some double forms are available, including one with white flowers.

G. psilostemon has vivid magenta flowers with black centres in summer; it forms big clumps of large, handsome leaves.

G. sanguineum, Bloody Cranesbill, has deeply cut leaves forming a mound about a foot (30 cm) high, and magenta purple flowers from mid- to late summer. 'Album' is a white form and 'Glenluce' is pink.

G. wallichianum has trailing stems and violet-blue flowers with white centres from mid-summer to autumn.

GEUM

G. rivale, Water Avens, is a plant for damp shade, not showy but pleasant. It has light green, scalloped leaves and hanging purplish flowers. 'Leonard's Variety' has pink flowers flushed with orange and 'Album' is white. It flowers in early summer.

GLAUCIDIUM

G. palmatum has four-petalled flowers 4 or 5 inches (10–12 cm) across, pinkish mauve with prominent stamens, and with two large, palmate leaves just below them. It may be as much as 4 feet (1·2 metres) tall. It is a Japanese native and is best in woodland conditions. There is a beautiful white form.

GUNNERA

G. magellanica is quite unlike the better known *G. manicata* with its huge leaves. This species has small round leaves with crinkly edges, not much more than 1 inch (2·5 cm) across, and spreads to form an attractive ground cover only a few inches high. The flowers are insignificant.

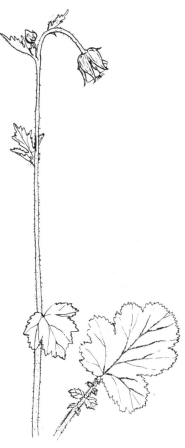

Geum rivale 'Album'

HABERLEA

H. rhodopensis has lilac flowers in spring and thick leaves with deeply impressed veins. *H. ferdinandi-coburgii* is very similar. Both are only a few inches high and are good for shady parts of a rock garden or crevices in a wall.

HELLEBORUS

This genus includes a number of useful shade lovers. They have attractive palmate leaves, sometimes evergreen. The flowers are not brightly coloured but are interesting and long-lasting.

H. atrorubens has purplish-green flowers from late winter to spring and grows about 1 foot (30 cm) tall.

H. corsicus has grey-green leaves with spiny margins that are evergreen. It has pale yellow-green flowers in early spring, about 2 feet (60 cm) tall.

H. foetidus, Stinking Hellebore, is an uncommon British native with handsome dark green deeply-cut leaves and clusters of hanging, pale green flowers edged with purple in winter and early spring. It is evergreen.

H. niger, the Christmas Rose, is the best-known species. It has hanging white flowers, usually tinged with pink, with prominent gold stamens, open in winter. It needs moist soil. The flowers tend to open rather close to the ground and to get splashed with mud. 'Potter's Wheel' is a fine form with large, pure white flowers held well clear of the ground.

H. orientalis, the Lenten Rose, is similar to the last, but the flowers vary in colour from pink to dull purple, often spotted inside. They flower from early winter to spring.

H. viridis is similar again but with green flowers.

HEMEROCALLIS

Day Lilies. They form large clumps of bright green, long, narrow arching leaves, with a succession of lily-like flowers over a long period in summer, on stalks 3–4 feet (around a metre) long. They do well in sun or partial shade and are very popular in Australia.

H. fulva has orange-brown flowers; its var. *rosea* has pink flowers.

Many garden hybrids are available as named cultivars with yellow, pink, apricot and copper flowers.

HEPATICA

H. triloba is a dwarf species related to Anemone with similar many-sepalled flowers, but with kidney-shaped, three-lobed leaves. The flowers open in early spring, and are typically mauve, but blue, pink and white varieties are available and also double forms. It is an attractive little plant for a shaded spot.

H. acutiloba and *H. americana* are American species similar to the last but with smaller flowers.

✕ HEUCHERELLA

A bigeneric hybrid between *Heuchera* and *Tierella*.

✕ *H. tiarelloides* spreads slowly in shade to form large clumps of round, evergreen leaves, and has 12-inch (30-cm) spikes of small, salmon-pink flowers in early summer. 'Bridget Bloom' has clear pink flowers.

HOSTA

The Plantain Lilies are among the most valuable of all shade-tolerant plants. There are many species and hybrids, some of the latter very much alike, and nomenclature is still somewhat confused. They seem to grow in any situation from sun to dense shade, and any soil from dry to moist. They are grown largely for their leaves, but the flowers are also attractive.

H. crispula has long, pointed undulating leaves edged with a broad band of white, and lilac flowers in late summer.

H. fortunei is a vigorous grower with broad green leaves and lilac flowers in late summer. There are a number of cultivars of this species:
'Albopicta' has leaves that, in spring, are yellow in the centre and green round the edge, gradually darkening to green all over.
'Albo-marginata' has leaves edged with white.
'Aurea' has leaves yellow in spring, turning green later.

'Aureo-marginata' has leaves edged with yellow.

H. lancifolia—dark green, glossy pointed leaves and lilac flowers.

H. rectifolia—plain green, broad leaves with impressed veins and deep lilac flowers; one of the best for flower effect.

H. sieboldiana has very broad, grey-green leaves, heavily veined, arranged in a regular whorled pattern round the crown, and pale lilac flowers. Var. *elegans* has even larger and bluer leaves. This is a spectacular plant—in my opinion, the best of all the Hostas.

H. sieboldii is quite different from the last; it has light green leaves with a white border.
'Thomas Hogg'—dark green leaves edged with white, and pale lilac flowers.

H. undulata has wavy, sometimes twisted, pointed leaves with a broad white patch in the centre and lilac flowers in summer.

H. ventricosa is a large species, with heart-shaped dark green leaves and deep lilac flowers.

HOUSTONIA

H. caerulea, Bluets, is an American species that grows in light, moist woodland. It grows only 2 or 3 inches (5–7 cm) high and has light green leaves and starry, pale blue flowers over a long period.

IRIS

Most of the irises are sun-lovers, but there are some that tolerate shade and they are useful for the shape of their sword-like leaves which contrasts with the broad or ferny leaves that most shade-lovers seem to have.

I. cristata is an American species only about 6 inches (15 cm) tall with pale mauve flowers with a yellow throat. Var. *lacustris* is even smaller.

I. foetidissima, Gladwyns, has evergreen leaves and grows in any position from sun to dense shade, even under trees. The flowers are not showy—yellow-purple—but are followed by large seed pods which split open into three sections, displaying orange-scarlet seeds. 'Chinese Form' is supposed to be bigger and better. 'Variegata' has leaves striped with white; it is very effective as a foliage plant but does not flower freely.

I. gracilipes has a creeping rootstock and lilac flowers with an orange flare, and leaves about a foot (30 cm) long.

JEFFERSONIA (PLAGIORHEGMA)

J. diphylla, Twinleaf, is an American woodland species with two leaves per plant, each divided into two segments, and white flowers with prominent yellow stamens on 6-inch (15-cm) stems in late spring.

J. dubia comes from Manchuria and has large, lavender flowers on stems 4–5 inches (10–12 cm) long in spring. The leaves are bronze when they first appear. These plants are related to Berberis and Epimedium, and both like a leafy soil.

KIRENGESHOMA

K. palmata has large, palmate leaves and 3-foot (1-metre) tall branched inflorescences with hanging, bright yellow flowers. It is native to Japan, and does well in woodland conditions with a humus-rich soil.

LAMIUM

The Dead-nettles are generally rather coarse plants, but some make useful and not unattractive ground-cover plants for shade.

L. galeobdolon 'Variegata' has evergreen, nettle-like leaves marbled with silvery white and yellow flowers in late spring/early summer. It grows about 1 foot (30 cm) tall and spreads rapidly—it can become rampant, but is useful under trees.

L. maculatum has leaves with a white stripe down the centre and purple-pink flowers. It, too, is evergreen, and is smaller than the last species—about 6 inches (15 cm) high. There are varieties with pink and white flowers. 'Aureum' has golden leaves, still with the white blotch, that scorch in hot sun.

LEUCOJUM

The Snowflakes are related to and rather similar to the Snowdrops, but are generally rather larger and have the six perianth segments equal in length.

L. aestivum, the Loddon Lily or Summer Snowflake, is rather oddly named as it flowers in spring. It has stout stems about 2 feet (60 cm) tall with a cluster of several pendant flowers at the tip—quite attractive, but the flowers always look too small for the size of the plant. It grows in shade or in the open if there is sufficient moisture.

Leucojum vernum

Leucojum aestivum

L. vernum, the Spring Snowflake, flowers in late winter and early spring, and again requires moisture. It is shorter, 8 or 9 inches (20–22 cm) high, and has larger flowers usually borne singly.

LILIUM

Many lilies are woodland plants but few, if any, tolerate dense shade. They often do best grown amongst shrubs such as deciduous azaleas, where the roots are shaded but the flowers can grow up into the sun. Many of the woodland species are of the Turk's Cap or Martagon type, whose flowers have strongly reflexed petals.

L. amabile, from Korea, is one of the Turk's Cap type, with deep orange flowers on 3-foot (1-metre) stems.

L. auratum, from Japan, is one of the finest of all lilies, with stems 6 feet (2 metres) tall or more and large, open flowers in late summer/early autumn, white with yellow or crimson spots. It is widely grown in New Zealand where conditions seem to suit it particularly well. It dislikes lime.

L. canadense is a very graceful species with yellow or orange bell-shaped flowers carried in whorls on a 5-foot (1·5-metre) stem. The leaves are also arranged in whorls. Var. *coccineum* has dark red flowers.

L. cernuum is another Korean species of the Martagon type, 2–3 feet (upto a metre) tall with lilac-pink flowers with darker spots.

L. davidii is supposed to be one of the easier species. It is a tall Turk's Cap species, with reddish-orange flowers on 5-foot (1·5-metre) stems in late summer.

L. hansonii is another fairly easy species, again of the Martagon type, with orange-yellow flowers spotted with brown on 5-foot (1·5-metre) stems.

L. humboldtii is a Californian woodland species with 6-foot (2-metre) stems bearing large, hanging Turk's Cap flowers, orange-red spotted with purple. The Bellingham Hybrids have been bred from this species; there are a number of named cultivars with orange or yellow flowers, all vigorous garden plants.

L. martagon is a variable European species with flowers ranging in colour from white to pinkish-purple and maroon. It usually grows 2–3 feet (up to a metre) high and may become naturalised in a woodland garden.

L. pardalinum, the Leopard or Panther Lily, comes from west North America. It has orange-red Turk's Cap flowers spotted with dark brown, on a 6-foot (2-metre) stem. It will grow in sun or partial shade, but must have plenty of moisture.

L. superbum is another handsome American Turk's Cap species, about the same height as the last, with yellow or orange flowers spotted with red in late summer. It too likes a moist soil.

LINNAEA

L. borealis, Twin Flower, is a British native that grows wild in pine woods on acid soil. It has long, trailing stems with small leaves and pink, bell-shaped flowers in pairs in summer. There is an American variety, var. *americana*, which is larger than the European form and is possibly a better garden plant.

LIRIOPE

L. muscari, Lily-turf, has stiff, grassy, evergreen leaves and spikes of violet-purple flowers from late summer to autumn. There is a white form, and I have seen one with white-bordered leaves which looked very attractive.

LUNARIA

L. biennis, Honesty, is one of those plants that seem to grow anywhere, in sun or shade. It has large, rather coarse, heart-shaped leaves and tall heads of magenta flowers in late spring, followed by the flat seed pods used so much in dried flower arrangements. Although it is biennial, it seeds itself freely if one does not pick all the seed heads. There is a white variety, and also an attractive variegated form, 'Variegata', that is supposed to come true from seed.

LUZULA

L. sylvatica (*maxima*), the Greater Woodrush, can be invasive and is not very exciting, but the form 'Marginata', which has leaves edged with white, is effective and useful in that it grows in dry shade.

LYSIMACHIA

L. nummularia, Creeping Jenny or Moneywort (Creeping Charlie, I believe, in the States), has starry yellow flowers and long trailing stems that can become invasive. 'Aurea' has golden foliage.

MAIANTHEMUM

M. bifolia has leaves in pairs rather like those of Lily-of-the-Valley, and small white flowers in late spring/early summer. It grows well in woodland conditions.

MECONOPSIS

These are aristocrats amongst herbaceous plants for light woodland or a shaded border. Many species are monocarpic, that is, the rosettes of leaves grow for several years until the plant reaches flowering size, and then, after flowering, the plant dies. They like cool, moist conditions—except for *M. cambrica*, which seems to grow anywhere—and tend to do better in cooler climates, in Scotland for example, where winter rot is less likely. They can be grown from seed, but the seedlings when small are very prone to damping off.

M. betonicifolia (*M. baileyi*) is the most widely grown of the Himalayan poppies. It has beautiful blue, poppy-like flowers with crinkly petals and yellow stamens; the plants usually flower in the second year after sowing and while some forms are true perennials, others behave like biennials.

M. cambrica, the Welsh Poppy, is a British native and much the easiest to grow, in fact once it is in a garden, it is there for ever as it sets seed prolifically. It has bright green, ferny leaves and clear yellow flowers borne

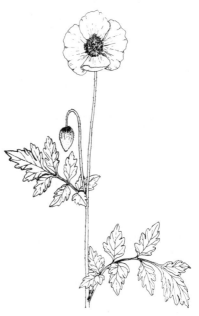

Meconopsis cambrica

singly on 12-inch (30-cm) stems that start to open at the beginning of summer and continue almost until autumn. There is an orange form but this is much less desirable. The plants are perennial with long tap roots and do not transplant too well unless very young. It grows in sun or shade.

M. dhwojii is one of the monocarpic species, with evergreen rosettes of divided leaves. The flowers are pale yellow, in tall inflorescences, and usually appear when the plant is three or four years old.

M. grandis is rather similar to *M. betonicifolia*, but has slightly larger flowers.

M. horridula has spiny leaves and stems and blue or blue-grey flowers. It is biennial.

M. integrifolia, the Lampshade Poppy, is only about a foot (30 cm) tall but has very large, yellow flowers. It usually dies after flowering.

M. nepaulensis is another monocarpic species, with decorative rosettes of deeply-cut leaves and tall inflorescences. The flowers are variable in colour—red, pink, white, yellow or even light blue.

M. quintuplinervia, the Harebell Poppy, has hanging, lavender flowers borne singly on stems about 2 feet (60 cm) tall.

M. regia has very striking rosettes of leaves covered with golden hairs and with serrated edges. Unfortunately they may rot in a mild, damp winter. The flowers are yellow, in tall inflorescences.

M. superba is very much like the last species, but with white instead of golden hairs on the foliage, and white flowers.

MERTENSIA

M. ciliata has blue, bell-shaped flowers in early summer; it is about 2 feet (60 cm) tall.

M. virginica, the Virginian Blue Cowslip, is related not to Primula but to Pulmonaria, which it rather resembles. The flowers open pink then turn blue, but the leaves are a glaucous blue-green and are not hairy.

MILIUM

M. effusum 'Aureum', Bowles' Golden Grass, is a form of the native Wood Millet. It grows 2 or 3 feet (up to a metre) tall and is bright gold in colour, particularly in spring.

MIMULUS

The Musks are showy plants, usually with a long flowering period, which spread rapidly. They grow in sun or partial shade, but must have plenty of moisture.

M. cardinalis has bright orange-scarlet funnel-shaped flowers in early summer and is less than a foot (30 cm) tall.

M. guttatus grows to about 18 inches (45 cm) and has yellow flowers spotted with red.

M. luteus, Yellow Musk, has large yellow flowers and is about 9 inches (22 cm) tall.

M. *ringens* is a tall species, up to 3 or 4 feet (around a metre), with violet flowers from mid- to late summer.

MISCANTHUS

M. sinensis is a non-invasive, clump-forming grass with panicles of pinkish-buff flowers in autumn, about 4 feet (1·2 metres) tall. It grows in sun or shade. It has two attractive cultivars: 'Variegatus', which has leaves with lengthwise white stripes, and 'Zebrinus', which is striped crosswise with yellow.

MOLINIA

M. caerulea 'Variegata' is a version of the native Purple Moor Grass. The leaves are striped longitudinally with white and the plumes of flower are purplish. It grows 12–18 inches (30–45 cm) high and likes a damp position.

NARCISSUS

In general, the daffodils are sun-lovers although many of the garden cultivars will grow and flower in light deciduous woodland.

N. cyclamineus does grow and become naturalised in partial shade. It is a delightful species, only 6–8 inches (15–20 cm) tall, with the petals completely turned back from the long, tubular corona. The flowers are rich yellow and open in early spring. It needs plenty of moisture in the soil.

N. pseudo-narcissus, the Lent Lily, is the English wild daffodil, with yellow trumpets and pale yellow outer segments. It will become naturalised in open woodland.

OMPHALODES

O. cappadocia has pointed green leaves and sprays of bright blue flowers like large forget-me-nots in late spring. It forms a good ground cover amongst shrubs; in an open position it seems liable to damage by spring frosts.

O. verna, Blue-eyed Mary, is similar but slightly smaller. Both like a cool situation.

Omphalodes verna

124

OURISIA

These are dwarf, creeping perennials from the southern hemisphere that dislike hot, dry situations.

O. caespitosa is very small, with grey-green leaves and clusters of white flowers in early summer, large for the size of the plant.

O. coccinea has red flowers and lobed leaves with deeply impressed veins.

O. macrocarpa has leaves with scalloped edges very reminiscent of those of an African Violet, and whorls of white flowers on stout stalks in early summer.

O. macrophylla is similar to the last species.

PAEONIA

Paeonies are often listed as plants that grow in shade as well as in sun. However, in my experience, both tree and herbaceous kinds need full sun if they are to flower properly, and do themselves poor justice in any sort of shade.

PELTIPHYLLUM

P. peltatum, American May Apple, has umbrella-like, lobed leaves and white flowers in late spring, followed by orange fruit. It grows about $1\frac{1}{2}$–2 feet (45–60 cm) tall, and needs a shaded situation.

P. emodi is a Japanese species whose leaves have three lobes.

PHALARIS

P. arundinacea 'Picta' is for some reason called Gardener's Garters. It has leaves with longitudinal white stripes and is very effective growing in sun or part shade. It can become invasive and should not be grown where it can smother anything choice. Occasional shoots may revert to green and these should be cut out.

POLEMONIUM

P. caeruleum, Jacob's Ladder, has lavender-blue flowers in early summer and pinnate leaves. It grows about 15 inches (38 cm) tall, in sun or light shade.

POLYGONATUM

P. multiflorum, Solomon's Seal, is an old cottage garden favourite, with arching stems 2–3 feet (up to a metre) high and greenish-white bell-shaped flowers hanging along their length in late spring/early summer. It prefers shade to sun and will grow in quite heavy shade, even under trees. 'Variegatum' has leaves bordered with white.

P. japonicum is very similar but slightly larger. It too has a variegated form.

P. verticillatum has leaves in whorls instead of alternately arranged, and straight rather than arching stems.

POLYGONUM

P. affine is a pleasant ground-cover

plant with spikes of pink flowers about 9 inches (22 cm) high from late summer until autumn. The leaves turn reddish-brown in winter and remain on the plant. 'Darjeeling Red' has red flowers. 'Donald Lowndes' is slightly more compact than the typical form. It grows in sun or partial shade.

P. macrophyllum is about 18 inches (45 cm) tall with narrow spikes of pink flowers from late summer to autumn. It likes a moist soil and does best in partial shade.

P. miletti is similar, but slightly earlier, with red flowers.

P. tenuicaule is another low-growing ground-cover species with spikes of white flowers in late spring, which prefers shade.

POTENTILLA

Most of the herbaceous potentillas prefer sun.

P. alba grows in sun or shade; it has evergreen, grey-green digitate leaves and white flowers with an orange eye in early spring and often again in autumn. It is only about 4 or 5 inches (10–12 cm) high.

PRIMULA

This is one of the most important genera for the shaded garden. As well as disliking heat, they must have plenty of moisture during the growing season; too much damp in winter, however, can result in the resting buds rotting. Another thing that can

happen in winter, which is more easily curable, is that the roots can be lifted from the ground by frost. It is worth checking on this every so often and firming any that have been loosened. Some species die back completely to below ground level in winter and do not suffer from these troubles. There are over five hundred species in the genus and quite a number of hybrids, so obviously it is impossible to mention here more than a small selection of those that adapt fairly well to garden conditions and are also more or less permanent. Most grow easily from seed and many will self-seed if conditions are to their liking. They are most effective planted in groups, or in drifts if space allows, rather than individually.

P. alpicola has umbels of hanging bell-shaped flowers on 18-inch (45-cm) stalks, in early summer. Typically they are pale yellow, but there are white and lilac forms.

P. anisodora is one of the Candelabra section—these have successive whorls of flowers opening along a longish stem. This is not one of the showiest, as the flowers are fairly small and very dark red in colour, usually with a yellow eye, but it often attracts attention because of the unusually dark flowers.

P. aurantiaca has whorls of orange-yellow flowers on stems 9–12 inches (22–30 cm) long.

P. beesiana is another of the Candelabra type, with pink-purple flowers with yellow eyes.

P. bulleyana has successive whorls of yellow flowers opening from red buds on stalks that are eventually about 18 inches (45 cm) tall. It is a particularly attractive species and dies back to below ground level in winter.

P. burmanica is rather like *P. beesiana*, but with deep purple flowers.

P. chionantha is one of the most beautiful species. It has distinctive long, narrow, light green leaves and clusters of scented white flowers, sometimes tinged with violet, in late spring. The dark calyces are sprinkled with white meal. It is sometimes said to die after flowering but I have found that it persists fairly well although it dies to below ground in winter and thus apparently vanishes.

P. denticulata, the Drumstick Primula or Easter Flower, has large, round heads of violet flowers on stiff stalks in spring. A number of colour forms are available, including purple-red and white. The leaves grow very large after flowering; this should be kept in mind when placing them. This species grows very vigorously in Scotland, but in southern England it tends to be tempted into too early growth and the flower buds may be caught by frost.

P. elatior, the Oxlip, has one-sided umbels of pale yellow flowers with some orange marks in the throat, open in late spring. It grows wild in woodland, like the primrose.

P. florindae is sometimes called the Giant Cowslip. It has large umbels of scented, pale yellow flowers in 3-foot (1-metre) stems from mid- to late summer. It is very vigorous and needs a moist situation; it does very well beside a pond or stream. It dies back to below ground in winter.

Primula florindae

P. geraniifolia has pretty, hairy leaves with scalloped edges and heads of lilac flowers on 9-inch (22-cm) stems. It is not a very vigorous species.

P. helodoxa is a tall species of the Candelabra type with bright yellow flowers in early summer on 3-foot (1-metre) stems.

P. involucrata has smallish, glossy leaves and heads of scented white flowers on 12-inch (30-cm) stems.

P. japonica is one of the easiest and most vigorous species with whorls of magenta flowers in early summer and rosettes of light green leaves that remain throughout the winter. There are pink and white forms—'Postford White' is particularly good.

P. nutans has hanging, violet-blue, bell-shaped flowers powdered with white, and narrow, hairy leaves. It does tend to die out after flowering but seed can be collected—it is so beautiful it must be mentioned.

P. prolifera is a vigorous candelabra-type species with bright yellow flowers in late spring.

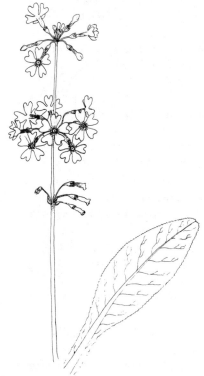

Primula pulverulenta

P. pulverulenta is an attractive and easily grown species, provided the site is not too dry. It has crimson flowers in whorls on 2-foot (60-cm) stems, with white meal on the calyces and stems. A number of forms and hybrids are available, such as 'Bartley Strain' and 'Inverewe Strain', with pink and apricot flowers.

P. rosea is one of the earliest to flower in spring, with shocking pink flowers that start to open as soon as they come through the soil, at the same time as the copper-coloured young leaves. The flower stalks gradually elongate to 5 or 6 inches (12–15 cm). Var. *grandiflora* has slightly larger flowers than the typical form.

P. secundiflora has one-sided umbels of drooping crimson-purple flowers on stalks about a foot (30 cm) tall.

P. sieboldii is a most attractive species, having pretty, light green leaves with scalloped edges and large, lilac flowers in early summer. There are also pink or white forms. In our garden it spreads freely, but is very susceptible to drought. The leaves die back very early in the year, in late summer.

P. sikkimensis is like a large cowslip, although it is not as big as *P. florindae*. It has scented yellow flowers in early summer.

P. sinopurpurea is rather like a violet-purple *P. chionantha*. The leaves are yellowish underneath. I have not grown it for long enough to know how perennial it is.

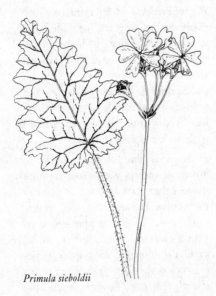

Primula sieboldii

P. viali is a striking and unusual-looking species with lilac flowers opening from scarlet bracts, so that the spike-like inflorescence is violet below and red above. The narrow leaves are densely furry. In Scotland, our plants persisted from year to year, but in the south of England it is much more difficult to keep them going, I suspect because of the milder, damper winters. It comes readily from seed, however.

P. vulgaris, the Primrose, is worth a place in any garden. Once established, it seeds itself freely. The subspecies *sibthorpii* has pink flowers. There are double forms, but any that I have seen have had flower heads too heavy for the stems so that the blooms lie on the ground.

P. yargongensis is rather like a pink-lilac version of *P. involucrata*.

POLYANTHUS

The hybrid primulas known as Polyanthus should also be mentioned here. These have umbels of large flowers in a great variety of colours—yellow, orange, red, pink and blue, usually with a yellow eye—from spring until mid-summer. They are very colourful and easy, as long as their position is not too hot or dry.

PULMONARIA

The lung-worts are useful ground cover plants for shade, growing in any soil with attractive, pointed and often spotted furry leaves.

P. angustifolia has bright blue flowers opening over a number of weeks from early to late spring. The leaves are dark green and sometimes faintly spotted.

P. officinalis, 'Soldiers and Sailors', has leaves conspicuously spotted with white. The flowers are pink when they first open in early spring and then turn blue.

P. rubra has lighter green leaves and dull red flowers, again in early spring.

P. saccharata is similar to the last but the leaves are larger, up to 1 foot (30 cm) long, and are more strikingly mottled with silver-white. 'Argentea' is a variety with even more silver colouring.

RANUNCULUS

R. aconitifolius 'Flore Pleno', Fair Maids of France, is a double buttercup with white, button-like flowers

Pulmonaria officinalis

in early summer, and deeply-cut leaves. It grows about 2 feet (60 cm) tall, in sun or partial shade, and must have a moist situation.

RHEUM

The ornamental rhubarbs are handsome foliage plants that do well beside water, or in woodland if it is sufficiently damp.

R. palmatum has large, heart-shaped leaves and tall panicles of deep red flowers in early summer, 6 feet (2 metres) high or more. 'Rubrum' is a variety with purple-red young growth which gradually fades from the tops of the leaves but remains underneath.

RODGERSIA

This is another genus grown mainly for its striking foliage, which again needs plenty of moisture. They are often planted near water, but I have seen them doing well in light woodland. They do best in partial shade.

R. aesculifolia has large, crinkly leaves tinged with bronze, shaped like those of a horse chestnut, as the name implies. The flowers are creamy-pink, in a feathery panicle about 4 feet (1·2 metres) tall, in late summer.

R. pinnata has pinnate leaves and white flowers. 'Superba' is a form with bronze leaves and pink flowers.

R. podophyllum has deeply-cut but not digitate leaves and creamy-white, feathery flowers.

R. tabularis has round, velvety, umbrella-like leaves and white flowers.

SANGUINARIA

S. canadensis, Bloodroot, has white flowers with many petals on very short stalks, and relatively large, lobed leaves. 'Flore Pleno' is a double form which, rather unusually, is greatly to be preferred. The flowers are the *whitest* I can think of, with no trace of another colour, neatly shaped, and they last longer than those of the single form. It flowers in spring. It is called Bloodroot because the root oozes red sap when damaged.

Saxifraga

This is a large genus, but most are alpines that need an open situation and so do not concern us here.

S. umbrosa, London Pride, has ever-green rosettes of leaves that spread rapidly, and panicles of small pink flowers in late spring/early autumn, not showy individually but giving an attractive, foamy effect in a mass. It is very suitable for edging a shaded border. 'Variegata' has leaves var-iegated with gold.

S. cuneifolia is related to the last species and is rather like it, but has white flowers.

S. fortunei has round leaves, purplish on the reverse, and loose panicles of white flowers from late summer to autumn.

Scilla

S. hyacinthoides has spikes of rather small, lilac-blue flowers in summer and broad, glossy leaves, up to 18 inches (45 cm) long. It grows best in woodland.

S. lilio-hyacinthus is very similar, but with slightly larger flowers.

S. sibirica has vivid blue flowers in early spring, three or four on an 8-inch (20-cm) stem. While it grows well in a sunny situation, it also seems to thrive in shade, for example under deciduous trees. There is a white form which is not so attractive. Var. *atrocaerulea* is usually slightly earlier.

Shortia

S. galacifolia is a beautiful North American woodland species with round, evergreen leaves with scal-loped edges, and hanging, pink or white bell-shaped flowers each on a single stalk in late spring. The leaves sometimes turn red in winter, although this is less marked in deep shade. It likes a damp, peaty soil.

S. uniflora is a Japanese species, equally beautiful. The pink flowers are slightly larger and more open than those of the last species, again with frilled petals. Both grow only about 6 inches (15 cm) high.

S. soldanelloides used to be put in a different genus, *Schizocodon*. The flowers are in one-sided racemes, not borne singly as in the last two species, and are bell-shaped, pink and mark-edly fringed.

Smilacina

S. racemosa is a graceful plant related to Solomon's Seal. It has similar arching stems, but the flowers are in a fluffy white head at the ends of the stems, in late spring. It likes a shady situation in lime-free soil.

Symphytum

S. grandiflorum, Comfrey, has rough green leaves and tubular pale yellow flowers in spring, opening from a coiled stem rather in the way that a fern-leaf unfurls. It spreads slowly and forms a dense ground cover even in heavy shade. It grows about 1 foot

(30 cm) tall. There are forms with blue or pink flowers.

TANAKAEA

T. radicans is related to Saxifrage. It is evergreen, with thick, leathery leaves and racemes of small white flowers about 10 inches (25 cm) high. Male and female flowers are borne on different plants; the former spreads by creeping stems while the latter does not. It grows best in damp shade.

TELLIMA

T. grandiflora forms spreading clumps of round, hairy evergreen leaves and has spikes of green bell-shaped flowers tinged with pink in late spring/early summer, 1–2 feet (30–60 cm) tall. It grows well under trees. 'Purpurea' has leaves that are purple below and turn purple-bronze in autumn and winter; the flowers are pink.

THALICTRUM

The Rues are grown mainly for their attractively divided leaves, reminiscent of those of Maidenhair Fern, and often grey-blue or grey-green in colour. Most are meadow plants but some will grow in shade.

T. aquilegifolium has fluffy white or lilac flowers from early to mid-summer, up to 4 feet (1·2 metres) tall. The name means 'leaves like a columbine', and this is an apt description.

T. diffusiflorum has lilac-blue flowers and grows about 18 inches (45 cm) tall.

TIARELLA

T. cordifolia, Foam Flower, has feathery spikes of white flowers about 1 foot (30 cm) tall. The leaves are evergreen, lobed and heart-shaped. It is a very pretty carpeting plant for shade.

T. wherryi is rather similar but more compact, with pale, almost yellow-green leaves and pink-tinged flowers.

TOLMIEA

T. menziesii, the Pick-a-back Plant, is often grown as a house-plant, but seems to do well outside in shade. The flowers are negligible; it is grown for its leaves which are shaped rather like those of Tiarella, but have young plantlets developing on top of them.

TRACHYSTEMON

T. orientalis has large, hairy leaves rather like those of Comfrey (to which it is related) that form a dense ground cover even in heavy shade. The flowers are blue with prominent yellow stamens, and open in spring, before the leaves enlarge.

TRICYRTIS

The Toad-lilies have curious, spotted flowers and like a cool, shaded situation.

T. hirta, the Japanese Toad Lily, has white flowers spotted with purple in late summer and early autumn. It grows about 1 foot (30 cm) tall.

T. macropoda has purple-spotted, yellowish flowers on 2-foot (60-cm) stems from mid-summer till early autumn.

T. stolonifera is slightly taller, with white flowers, again spotted with purple, from late summer to autumn.

TRILLIUM

These are easily grown and very attractive woodland plants. There are many species, native to North America, Japan, China and the Himalayas; I am mentioning some of those that are more readily available. All have three-petalled flowers.

T. cernuum has three round leaves forming a sort of umbrella, with the flower-stalk coming from the point of junction and bending over. The flowers are pink or white. This species grows about 1 foot (30 cm) tall.

T. erectum has red flowers open in late spring/early summer, and is 12–15 inches (30–40 cm) tall.

T. grandiflorum, Wake Robin, has large, white flowers held well above the foliage. It grows about 1 foot (30 cm) tall and has the largest flowers of the genus, 2 or 3 inches (5–7 cm) across. 'Roseum' is a pink form and 'Flore Plenum' has double flowers.

T. luteum has yellow flowers tinged with green and grows only about 6 inches (15 cm) high. It flowers in summer.

T. nivale is one of the earliest to flower, in spring. It is another dwarf species, and has white flowers.

T. sessile has mottled leaves and dark red, stalkless flowers in spring.

TROLLIUS

The globe-flowers grow in sun or shade, but must have moisture. The leaves are divided and buttercup-like.

T. acaulis is only about 6 inches (15 cm) high and has bright golden yellow flowers in summer.

T. chinensis has large, golden flowers in summer and grows about 1 foot (30 cm) high.

T. europaeus has lemon yellow flowers and glossy leaves; it grows to about 2½ feet (75 cm).

T. pumilus is another dwarf species, 6–12 inches (15–30 cm) high, with golden flowers in summer.

UVULARIA

U. grandiflora is a graceful woodland plant, with arching stems, rather like Solomon's Seal, but with much larger, drooping yellow flowers that open in late spring/early summer.

VANCOUVERIA

V. hexandra comes from west North America and, in the wild, grows in woodland in deep shade. It is related to Epimedium and must have an acid, humus-rich soil. The leaves are finely divided and it has starry yellow flowers in early summer.

VERATRUM

V. album has panicles of greenish-white flowers on 3-foot (1-metre) stems in late summer, and large leaves.

V. nigrum has almost black flowers.

VIOLA

Most of the garden pansies and violas do well even in quite heavily shaded borders. There is no point in listing the many cultivars and colour-forms available.

V. cornuta has bright green leaves and pale blue-violet flowers on long stalks throughout the summer. There are white and purple forms.

V. glabella has yellow flowers and heart-shaped leaves and will grow under trees.

WALDSTEINIA

W. ternata has dark, evergreen, lobed leaves and trailing stems that root as they go so that it soon makes a dense ground cover, only a few inches high. It has five-petalled yellow flowers in late spring.

8

Climbers and Wall Plants

This is rather a mixed bag of plants, some self-clinging climbers and some rather straggly growers that are better fixed to a wall. All either must have shade or will grow in shade, which of course includes a shaded wall.

ACTINIDIA

A. chinensis, the Chinese Gooseberry, is a twining plant with large, heart-shaped leaves and stems covered with reddish hairs. The flowers are creamy yellow, in spring, and after a good summer are followed by edible fruits looking rather like elongated gooseberries, about 2 inches (5 cm) long. It does well in Australia and New Zealand, where selected fruiting clones are available. It can reach about 30 feet (9 metres) in height.

AKEBIA

A. quinata is semi-evergreen, with twining stems which again can reach 30 feet (9 metres) or more. The leaves have five leaflets; the flowers are reddish and open in spring, and after a good summer may be followed by long, purple fruits.

A. trifoliata has leaves with three leaflets and light violet-purple fruit. Both come from Japan and China.

ARISTOLOCHIA

These are twining plants that grow in sun or shade.

A. macrophylla, Dutchman's Pipe, has large, heart-shaped leaves and tubular flowers bent upwards near the base like a U-tube, yellow and purple-brown in colour. These are produced in mid-summer. It comes from east North America and can grow to about 20 feet (6 metres).

A. sempervirens originates from North Africa and the Mediterranean and so is much less hardy, although it usually comes again from the roots even if the top growth is killed. It is evergreen, with flowers similar to the last. It needs to be tied to its supports.

ASTERANTHERA

A. ovata is a trailing plant that likes damp, shady woodland conditions; it does splendidly in the west of the British Isles where it climbs up tree trunks and trails over rocks and banks. It has tubular flowers in pairs, about 1 inch (2·5 cm) long and brilliant red, and small, furry green leaves. In hot areas, woodland or a shaded wall is essential. It comes from Chile.

BERBERIDOPSIS

B. corallina also must have a shaded position, and a moist, lime-free soil. It has leathery evergreen leaves with spiny margins and deep red flowers in late summer. It can reach 15 feet (4 metres). It is a very handsome plant, again native to Chile.

BERCHEMIA

These are twining climbers with insignificant flowers but pleasant foliage; they grow in sun or part shade.

B. racemosa has leaves 5 or 6 inches (12–15 cm) long with parallel veins, that turn yellow in autumn. 'Variegata' has leaves marked with white.

CELASTRUS

C. orbiculatus is a vigorous, twining climber that will reach 30 or 40 feet (9–12 metres) covering an old tree. The stems are spiny; the leaves are roundish and turn yellow in autumn. The flowers are insignificant, but the seed capsules when they split open are yellow inside and contain bright red seeds. It is important to have a hermaphrodite form so that fruits will develop; some plants are unisexual. There are several other, rather similar species in the genus, but this is the free-est fruiting.

CLEMATIS

Most of the clematis like full sun, although they need a cool root-run.

C. montana, however, will grow on a shaded wall. It is a vigorous, not to say rampant, species, that can grow to 30 feet (9 metres) or more. It looks very well scrambling over an old tree. It has white flowers about 1½ inches (4 cm) in diameter in early summer. A number of cultivars are available. Var. *grandiflora* is even more vigorous, with slightly larger flowers. Var. *rubens* has pink flowers and bronze new growth. 'Elizabeth' and 'Tetrarose' are both pink and larger-flowered, the latter with bronze-tinged foliage.

DECUMARIA

D. barbara is a self-clinging climber related to Hydrangea which will climb for 20 feet (6 metres) or so up a wall or tree trunk. It comes from the southern United States and is semi-evergreen, with leaves up to 6 inches (15 cm) long and small white flowers in summer.

EUONYMUS

E. fortunei is a self-clinging climber with evergreen leaves about 2 inches (5 cm) long. It can be used as a ground cover in sun or shade, but seems then to grow much more slowly and is not very satisfactory. Var. *radicans*, which has slightly smaller leaves, is the kind most often grown especially in one of the variegated forms. There are a number of these which are all really rather similar: 'Silver Pillar' has a fairly upright habit and white bordered leaves; 'Silver Queen' has broad yellowish margins to the leaves and 'Variegatus' has creamy yellow variegation, sometimes pink-flushed. The climbing shoots do not produce flowers, but they are sometimes borne by the shrubby growth at the bottom of the plant, particularly after a hot summer. The flowers are insignificant and greenish, but the fruits are quite decorative in a small way, pink capsules with orange seeds inside. The plant can easily reach 10 or 12 feet (3–3·6 metres), and probably more if space were available.

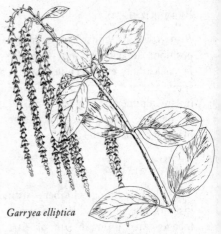

Garryea elliptica

They transplant badly and so should be moved into their permanent position when quite young.

GARRYA

These are evergreen shrubs with male and female catkins on separate plants. They are not in any way climbers, but are almost always grown against a wall, usually a shaded wall, so I have included them here. They grow on any well-drained soil and are very tolerant of atmospheric pollution. There are a number of species, but the following (which is the most often grown) is both the hardiest and the most effective.

G. elliptica has grey-green catkins 6 inches (15 cm) long or more on the male plant—the female ones are barely 3 inches (7·5 cm) long. These flowers appear in late winter and early spring. They grow usually 8–10 feet (2·4–3 metres) high and if a plant has to be cut back, this should be done immediately after flowering.

HEDERA

The ivies are probably the best-known and most widely used of all climbing plants. They grow in any soil and situation and are tolerant of atmospheric pollution. They can be used as a ground cover under trees where the shade is too dense for almost anything else—wild ivy often grows in this way.

H. helix is the Common Ivy, or English Ivy. The climbing shoots have lobed leaves; the fertile shoots, which are shrubby in character, have ovate leaves. Many cultivars are available; I shall list only a few.

'Buttercup' is probably the best yellow form. The leaves are smallish and are bright yellow in spring, but turn greener as the summer goes on. 'Cristata' has leaves crinkly at the margin.

'Glacier' has grey-green leaves, edged with white.

'Gold Heart' has small leaves with a heart-shaped splash of yellow in the centre of the leaf. It is much less vigorous than the typical form—this would apply to all the variegated forms.

'Marginata' has leaves with a broad white edging, sometimes flushed with pink.

H. canariensis, Canary Island Ivy, has large leaves, up to 6 inches (15 cm) long and broad, sometimes slightly three-lobed. The form 'Variegata', also known as 'Gloire de Marengo', is the one most often grown. It has leaves marked with grey-green and edged with white. It is sometimes damaged by frost, but usually comes away rapidly in spring. This is more likely to happen if it is grown on a fence rather than a wall, where it gets more protection.

H. colchica, Persian Ivy, is similar, with leaves perhaps slightly larger— I find them very difficult to tell apart. 'Dentata Variegata' is similar to *H. canariensis* 'Variegata' but is supposed to be hardier.

HYDRANGEA

See also p. 86. Three species of climbing hydrangea are in cultivation; all are self-clinging, with aerial roots like ivy and grow in sun or shade—they do well on shaded walls and also climbing up the trunks of trees.

H. petiolaris is most often grown. It has toothed, heart-shaped leaves and bright brown stems which make a decorative tracery in winter. The flowers open in summer; they are in flat heads with some large, white sterile florets round the edge, like the lace-caps. It can climb 60 feet (18 metres) or more into a tree.

H. anomala is rather similar but less vigorous, not usually reaching more than 30 or 40 feet (9–12 metres)!

H. integerrima is evergreen, with panicles of flowers in late summer.

JASMINUM

J. nudiflorum is not really a climber, but its long stems are so floppy that they need the support of a wall or fence. It has bright yellow flowers on the bare branches from mid-winter to early spring. Technically, it is deciduous, with small, trifoliate leaves, but the stems are bright green. If it needs tidying up, it can be cut back after flowering; it stands clipping surprisingly well.

J. polyanthum is an evergreen Chinese species with strongly scented white flowers, tinged with pink on the outside, open throughout the summer. It does very well in Australia and tolerates some shade there, but in Britain it is hardy out of doors only in a sunny spot in a mild area.

J. suavissimum is an Australian species that likes similar climatic conditions to the last. Again, it has heavily scented white flowers.

LONICERA

The honeysuckles are amongst the most popular of all climbers. Some species like sun, but others are naturally found in woodland.

L. × *americana* (known as Italian honeysuckle!) will tolerate some shade. It has whorls of long, tubular, creamy-yellow flowers stained with purple and heavily scented, in summer.

L. caprifolium has whorls of scented, creamy-yellow, pink-tinged flowers in summer. It is similar in flower to *L. periclymenum*, but the upper leaves are perfoliate— that is to say, a pair of leaves is joined so that the stem seems to grow through the middle.

L. japonica var. *halliana*, Japanese honeysuckle, is an extremely vigorous evergreen or semi-evergreen species. It has pairs of white flowers, turning yellow as they age, very sweetly scented, from mid-summer until autumn. It grows well in sun or shade. 'Aureoreticulata' has leaves with a gold network.

L. periclymenum, Woodbine or Common Honeysuckle, has whorls of scented, creamy-yellow flowers sometimes tinged with pink outside, from mid- to late summer and early autumn, followed by red berries. 'Belgica', known as Early Dutch, has

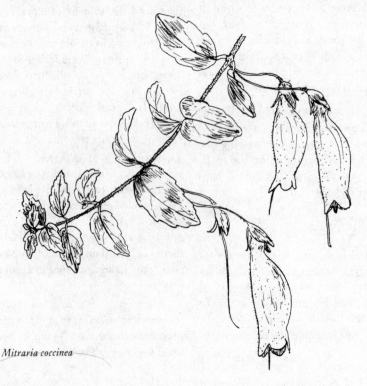

Mitraria coccinea

flowers more strongly marked with purple in early summer, and often again in autumn. 'Serotina', Late Dutch, is almost identical to the last mentioned, but starts to flower in mid-summer.

L. × tellmaniana has large clusters of orange-yellow flowers opening from red buds in summer. The upper leaves are perfoliate. It is particularly good in shade.

L. tragophylla must have shade, and thrives in dense shade. It has clusters of yellow flowers in summer.

MITRARIA

M. coccinea, from Chile, has small, shiny leaves and large, tubular vermilion flowers, sprinkled with a sort of glittery down, from early to late summer. It prefers a lime-free soil and a moist, cool, shaded situation in a mild area, where it can climb up a tree-trunk or trail down a bank.

PARTHENOCISSUS

These used to be classified under *Vitis*.

P. henryana is self-clinging and has digitate leaves with either three or five leaflets, sometimes tinged with bronze, and with a network of white veins. The leaves turn red in autumn.

P. quinquefolia, Virginia Creeper, is another self-clinging species. It is extremely vigorous and has leaves with five leaflets which turn red in autumn.

P. tricuspidata, Boston Ivy, is the plant usually known as Virginia Creeper in Britain. It is distinguished from the true Virginia Creeper by having leaves that are three-lobed and not digitate. It is self-clinging, very vigorous, and tolerant of atmospheric pollution. The leaves turn a brilliant red in autumn.

PILEOSTEGIA

P. viburnoides is an evergreen, self-clinging climber, related to Hydrangea, that grows in sun or shade, and does very well on a shaded wall. It has leathery leaves about 6 inches (15 cm) long and panicles of creamy-white flowers from late summer to autumn.

POLYGONUM

P. aubertii must, along with the next species, be one of the most rapidly growing plants in cultivation, certainly in a temperate climate. It is a rampant grower and should not be planted near anything choice, but is useful for screening purposes. It has large panicles of greenish-white flowers in summer.

P. baldschuanicum, Russian Vine, is equally rampant and is similar to the last species, but the flowers are tinged with pink.

PYRACANTHA

The Firethorns are not really climbers and can be trained as free-standing bushes, but they are usually grown against walls. Although they are grown mainly for their berries, the heads of white, hawthorn-like flowers in late spring/early summer are quite decorative, and they are all evergreen. They are not fussy about soil and do well on shaded walls—the berries are then slower to ripen than when the plant gets more sun, but on the other hand, they last longer.

P. atlantioides is often sold as *P. gibbsii*. It can be trained to form a tree of up to 20 feet (6 metres), and against a wall it covers a large area. Long shoots that are not wanted can be cut out at any time. The red berries are long-lasting. 'Aurea' has deep yellow fruit.

P. coccinea flowers in summer and has masses of red berries in autumn and winter. 'Lalandei' is a more vigorous and upright form, with larger berries.

P. rogersiana has orange-red fruit, freely produced, and can grow quite large. 'Flava' has bright yellow berries. 'Watereri' (*P. atlantioides* × *P. rogersiana*) is compact, with flowers and red berries freely produced.

ROSA

Quite a number of climbing and rambling roses will grow satisfactorily on a shaded wall, as long as there is sufficient direct light and good circulation of air—probably many more than I have listed here.

R. filipes 'Kiftsgate'—extremely vigorous, needs plenty of space; single white flowers in large clusters in summer, not recurrent; grey-green foliage.

'Alberic Barbier'—creamy-white double flowers tinged with pale yellow in mid-summer; dark, glossy foliage.

'Conrad F. Meyer'—silvery pink, scented flowers in early summer, with some flowers afterwards.

'Danse du Feu'—vermilion-red, long flowering period.

'Dr Van Fleet'—pale pink, scented, free-flowering in mid-summer.

'Félicité et Perpetué'—small, scented, creamy-white flowers in summer; vigorous—can reach 20 feet (6 metres).

'Hugh Dickson'—light crimson, scented and recurrent; very vigorous.

'Gloire de Dijon'—buff-yellow, scented; recurrent.

'Lady Waterlow'—salmon pink, scented, recurrent.

'Mme Alfred Carrière'—white, recurrent.

'Mme Caroline Testout'—bright pink, full flowers.

'Mme Grégoire Staechelin'—deep pink, large flowers, very fragrant; mid-summer.

'Maigold'—clusters of large, semi-double, fragrant yellow flowers.

'Mermaid'—very large, single, pale yellow flowers with prominent golden stamens opening over many months; glossy, evergreen foliage; very vigorous and disease-resistant.

'Parkdirektor Riggers'—single, scar-

let flowers over a long season.
'Paul's Scarlet Climber'—clusters of double, scarlet flowers in summer; liable to black spot.
'Zéphirine Drouhin'—carmine-pink, scented flowers; thornless.

SCHIZOPHRAGMA

Yet another genus of self-clinging climbers related to Hydrangea.

S. hydrangeoides is similar to *Hydrangea petiolaris*, with flat heads of creamy-white flowers and yellowish bracts in summer. It can reach 40 feet (12 metres) in height. The leaves are roundish and toothed. 'Roseum' has the bracts tinged with pink.

S. integrifolium is similar, but has pointed leaves, only slightly toothed, and larger flowers and bracts.

TRACHELOSPERMUM

Very attractive, twining plants with scented flowers in late summer. In temperate climates, they are hardy only in a mild district and would be better in a sunny spot, but they are widely grown in Australia where they will tolerate some shade.

T. asiaticum is a Japanese species with dark, glossy leaves and creamy flowers that turn yellow as they age.

T. jasminoides will grow to about 23 feet (7 metres) in height. The flowers are white, turning to cream.

VITIS

V. coignetiae is a self-clinging climber with spectacular, heart-shaped leaves as much as a foot (30 cm) across, rusty-brown below, turning brilliant red in autumn. It can reach 60 feet (18 metres) in height.

9

Ferns

Ferns are indispensable plants for the shaded garden; many will grow in shade too dense for any flowering plant. Many more species and varieties are available than most people imagine—I am giving a selection of these. Furthermore, in any country, native ferns will usually adapt well to garden conditions, although care must be taken not to uproot rare species. In Australia, many species that in Britain are grown as indoor plants, for example species of *Pteris* and *Platycerium*, the Stag's Horn Fern, can be grown out of doors.

Ferns are difficult to describe without going into botanical detail, and so I shall just give size, preferred conditions and any particular characteristics. A further complication is that the nomenclature has been changed a great deal—for example, the Beech Fern, *Thelypteris phegopteris*, has been known variously as *Dryopteris phegopteris*, *Polypodium phegopteris*, and *Phegopteris polypodioides*! It is by no means impossible that in the future it will be changed yet again.

ADIANTUM

The Maidenhair ferns are amongst the most beautiful species, usually with black, glossy leaf-stalks and finely divided leaves with fan-shaped segments. There are about two hundred species, mostly tropical and warm temperate, but the following are hardy provided a shaded, fairly moist position is provided.

A. capillus-veneris is a rare British native, with leaves 6–12 inches (15–30 cm) long.

A. pedatum is a beautiful species with light-green fronds, 1½–2 feet (45–60 cm) long.

A. venustum is a Himalayan species that seems to be fairly hardy.

ASPLENIUM

A. ruta-muraria, Wall Rue Spleenwort, is widely distributed in Europe, Asia and North America. It has leaves less than 6 inches (15 cm) long, with few segments.

A. trichomanes, Maidenhair Spleenwort, has simply pinnate leaves with dark leaf-stalks, usually about 6 inches (15 cm) long but sometimes slightly more. Both of these species are very tolerant of drought and will grow in shady walls and rock crevices.

ATHYRIUM

A. filix-foemina, Lady Fern, has finely divided leaves, 3 feet (a metre) tall or more. It likes a fairly moist situation.

Var. *minutissima* is a dwarf version with a creeping rhizome that will grow in dense shade. Var. *rubellum* has pink stems.

BLECHNUM

B. penna-marina is a mat-forming fern from New Zealand. It can be clipped back in spring to show off the bronze tips of the new growth.

B. spicant, the Hard Fern, has sterile and fertile fronds. Both are simply pinnate and stiff in texture. The fertile leaves are in the centre of the clump and stand erect, and look brownish when they are covered with spores; the sterile leaves are round the outside, and are more spreading, about 18 inches (45 cm) long. It dislikes lime.

B. tabulare is a South African native that nevertheless is able to survive quite hard frost. The new growth is pinkish, turning dark green later on. It is about 2 feet (60 cm) tall.

CETERACH

C. officinarum, the Rustyback Fern, has simply pinnate leaves, up to 8 inches (20 cm) long, covered with rusty-brown scales beneath. In the wild, it grows in cracks in limestone rocks and in walls; it tolerates dry conditions and dense shade.

DENNSTAEDTIA

D. punctiloba, the Hay-scented Fern, has feathery, pale green leaves that are sweetly scented. It spreads vigorously, but less so if it is grown in a dry situation.

DICKSONIA

D. antarctica is a magnificent tree fern, coming from New Zealand and Australia, which has a trunk up to perhaps 10 feet (3 metres) tall with whorls of long, divided leaves at the top. In Britain it is hardy only in the south-west, but grows well in Australia and New Zealand if given shade. *Cyathea australis* is another tree fern species that is often grown in Australia, rather more drought-resistant than Dicksonia.

DRYOPTERIS

This is a large genus, with about 150 species, found in Europe, Asia and America. The various species form large clumps, but do not spread very much.

D. carthusiana, the Narrow Buckler Fern, has handsome leaves up to 4 feet (1·2 metres) long and likes a fairly moist position.

D. cristata, the Crested Buckler Fern, has fairly upright leaves, 3-3½ feet (a metre) long and also likes a damp situation.

D. filix-mas, the Male Fern, is one of the commonest British ferns. It is 3 or 4 feet (around a metre) tall and grows easily in almost any situation. Var. *polydactyla* has fronds ending in a sort of crest.

D. marginalis is a vigorous, evergreen American species.

MATTEUCCIA

M. struthiopteris, the Ostrich Fern or Shuttlecock Fern, forms large crowns with symmetrically arranged fronds. It grows about 3 feet (a metre) tall and likes a moist situation.

ONOCLEA

O. sensibilis, the Sensitive Fern, is a very attractive species native to North America and northern Asia, with pale fronds and a creeping rhizome. It grows 12–18 inches (45–60 cm) high and needs a fair bit of moisture.

OSMUNDA

O. cinnamomea is an American species with the young growth covered by rusty-brown scales.

O. regalis, the Royal Fern, is much the largest of the British ferns, growing up to 6 feet (2 metres) tall. The spore-bearing parts of the leaves are concentrated at the tips of the fronds, rather like a flower-head. It likes a damp situation.

PHYLLITIS

P. scolopendrium, Hart's Tongue Fern, has simple, strap-shaped leaves, unlike those generally thought of as 'ferny'. It grows about 1–1½ feet (45–60 cm) tall, in any situation including heavy shade. Var. *ramo-*

cristata is smaller, with undulating fronds, crested at the tips.

POLYPODIUM

P. vulgare, Common Polypody, grows almost anywhere, in any soil or position, including dry shade. In the wild, it is often seen as an epiphyte, growing on the forks of trees. The leaves are simply pinnate, about 1 foot (30 cm) long.

POLYSTICHUM

P. acrostichoides, Christmas Fern, is a very hardy American species with evergreen forms about 1½ feet (45 cm) long.

P. aculeatum, Hard Shield Fern, has evergreen fronds, rigid in texture, dark green above and paler below, about 2 feet (60 cm) long.

P. lonchitis, Holly Fern, has simply pinnate leaves with the edges toothed, again stiff in texture, about 1½ feet (45 cm) long.

P. setiferum, Soft Shield Fern, has soft, arching fronds about 3 feet (a metre) long.

THELYPTERIS

This genus seems to have suffered more than most from name changes, and some of the older ones still appear in catalogues.

T. dryopteris, the Oak Fern, has been known by at least four other names. The fronds are much divided and bracken-like, but it is a much smaller plant than bracken, only 12–18 inches (45–60 cm) high, and is not invasive although it has a creeping rhizome. It does not like too dry a site.

T. palustris, Marsh Fern, also has a creeping rhizome. The leaves are borne singly, or occasionally there are a few in a tuft, about 2 feet (60 cm) long. It does best in a very damp situation.

T. phegopteris, Beech Fern, has a creeping rhizome and solitary, finely divided leaves 9–18 inches (22–45 cm) long. It likes a moist situation.

WOODWARDIA

W. virginica, Virginian Chain Fern, has arching fronds about 2 feet (60 cm) long which are bronze when they first appear.

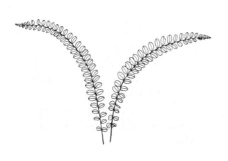

Asplenium trichomanes

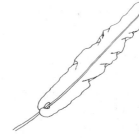

Phyllitis scolopendrium

Dryopteris filix-mas

Polypodium vulgare

10

Miscellaneous

This chapter includes notes on various groups of plants which do not seem to fit in elsewhere, but are nevertheless of interest.

BAMBOOS

Bamboos always give a rather exotic look to a garden and not all species are rampant growers, as is often thought. They are very difficult to tell apart, in many cases, but here is a small selection of some that should grow well in a shaded garden.

ARUNDINARIA

A. graminea has very narrow leaves and can grow up to about 10 feet (3 metres) tall.

A. hindsii is a vigorous grower, up to 11 or 12 feet (over 3 metres) in height. It grows in sun or shade.

A. humilis is only about 4 feet (1·2 metres) high, but spreads rapidly. It grows in shade, even below trees.

A. nitida is a very handsome species with graceful leaves and purple-tinged canes. It forms large clumps but does not spread too much, and reaches about 12 feet (3·6 metres) in height.

A. spathiflora is another clump-forming species, growing from 10 to 15 feet (3–4 metres) tall. Again, the canes are tinged with purple.

A. vagans is only 2 or 3 feet (up to a

metre) high but is a rampant grower. It thrives even in dense shade.

A. viridistriata has leaves striped with green and yellow that retain their coloration in shade. It grows 4–6 feet (1·2–2 metres) tall.

CHUSQUEA

C. couleou has dark green canes about 10 feet (3 metres) high, with short leafy branches. It forms large clumps, and I have seen it growing under tall shade. The stems are solid, not hollow as in almost all other bamboos.

PHYLLOSTACHYS

P. aurea is a graceful species 10–12 feet (3–3·6 metres) high. The name 'aurea' appears to refer to the yellowish colour of the mature canes and not to foliage colour.

P. viridi-glaucescens forms large clumps and grows up to 18 feet (5 metres) tall. The leaves are bright green above and pale below.

SASA

S. veitchii is a low-growing species, forming large clumps 3–4 feet (around a metre) tall. The leaves are relatively short and broad—8–10 inches long by 1–2 inches across (20–25 cm by 2·5–5 cm). In autumn, the leaf edges wither and become whitish, giving a variegated effect throughout winter.

ANNUALS

Most annuals like as much sun as possible, but there are a few that grow in shade and are useful if some colour is wanted quickly.

Asperula azurea setosa, Annual Woodruff, has clusters of scented pale blue flowers over a long period in summer. It grows about 1 foot (30 cm) tall. It is hardy and can be sown outside from mid- to late spring.

Calceolaria rugosa. These are half-hardy annuals that should be sown in a greenhouse from late winter to mid-spring and can be planted out when the risk of frost is past. They grow in sun or shade and have the usual pouched calceolaria flower, generally in shades of yellow or orange-brown. They grow about 12 inches (30 cm) high.

Clarkia elegans has 2-foot (60-cm) stems with double flowers, pink, white, red or mauve, scattered along their lengths. It can be sown outside from mid- to late spring and grows in sun or light shade.

Cynoglossum amabile, Hound's Tongue, has turquoise blue flowers like large forget-me-nots in late summer and furry grey-green leaves. It grows about 18 inches (45 cm) tall; the seeds should be sown outside in mid-spring.

Impatiens. These are sometimes grown in Britain, but are widely grown in the States, particularly in shade where other colourful annuals such as Petunias do not thrive. The Imp and Elfin strains were developed from *I. walleriana*, a South African species. These come in a wide range of colours—pink, salmon, orange, red, purple and white—and vary in height from 6 to about 15 inches (15–40 cm). The flowers may be as much as 2½ inches (7·5 cm) across. Older groups of hybrids, such as Baby and Jewel, have a less wide colour range, but are still good plants. A few bicolours and doubles are available. Some new varieties of Impatiens originating in the Far East are on the market in America but not, as far as I know, in the British Isles. These often have multi-coloured leaves—red and yellow on green.

Impatiens are half-hardy annuals and should be sown in a heated greenhouse in mid-spring.

Lobelia erinus is the popular edging Lobelia. The species has blue and white flowers, but a great many cultivars are available with flowers ranging from pale to very deep blue. They grow in sun or shade and should be sown in a greenhouse in mid-spring and planted out towards the beginning of summer.

Mimulus cupreus, Monkey Flower, requires a moist position in sun or shade. It grows about 9 inches (22 cm) high and has large, trumpet-shaped flowers in yellow, orange or red. A number of named varieties are available.

Nemophila insignis has bright blue flowers with white centres from midsummer on, and pretty, feathery foliage. It grows about 9 inches (22 cm) high and must have a cool, damp position. It can be sown outside from mid- to late spring.

Tropaeolum canariense, the Canary Creeper, is a very attractive climbing plant with bright yellow flowers over a long period and fresh green foliage. It can also be used to trail from window boxes or hanging baskets. It can be sown in late spring in open ground, or earlier in a greenhouse.

FRUIT AND VEGETABLES

Where these are concerned, we must accept that shade is a drawback. If at all possible, a sunny area should be set aside for the vegetable garden and if this cannot be done, it is not a case of choosing varieties that prefer shade but rather of selecting ones that will survive and produce something in these conditions.

We have found that the following will give a reasonable return in a plot that is shaded for most of the day.
Potatoes
Lettuce
Broad beans
French beans
Runner beans
Rhubarb
Strawberries
Gooseberries
Blackcurrants
Redcurrants

Morello cherries are usually grown on shaded walls. This is a sour cherry, although when fully ripe it can be used as a dessert fruit. It is the most suitable of the fruiting cherries for the average garden, as not only is it a less vigorous grower than the sweet cherries, but it is self-fertile and so only one tree need be planted. The training and pruning of Morello cherries is quite complex, and anyone intending to grow one should consult a book about fruit-growing.

Appendix

Sarcococca spp.
Symphoricarpus rivularis
Vaccinium ovatum
Xanthorrhiza simplicissima

HERBACEOUS PLANTS

Actaea spp.
Ajuga reptans
Anemone × hybrida
A. vitifolia
Arisaema triphyllum
Arisarum proboscideum
Asperula odorata
Cardamine asarifolia
C. trifolia
Convallaria majalis
Cyclamen spp.
Digitalis spp.
Epimedium spp.
Euphorbia amygdaloides
Geranium nodosum
Helleborus foetidus
Hosta spp.
Iris foetidissima
Lameum galeobdolon
Lathraea clandestina
Lunaria biennis
Polygonatum spp.
Symphytum grandiflorum
Trachystemon orientalis
Vancouveria hexandra

PLANTS THAT WILL TOLERATE DRY SHADE

Asperula odorata
Buxus sempervirens
Chimaphila maculata
Convallaria majalis
Cyclamen spp.

Digitalis spp.
Gaylussacia brachycera
Hedera spp.
Helleborus foetidus
H. orientalis
Hypericum calycinum
H. × moseranum
Lunaria biennis
Luzula sylvatica 'Marginata'
Mahonia aquifolium
Ruscus spp.
Sarcococca spp.
Saxifraga umbrosa
Symphoricarpus rivularis
Vinca spp.

PLANTS FOR WINDOW-BOXES IN SHADE

Campanula isophylla
Euonymus fortunei radicans
Fuchsias
Hedera spp.
Impatiens
Lobelia erinus
Polyanthus
Rhododendron (dwarf spp. and hybrids, including azaleas)
Sarcococca spp.
Vinca minor

Most dwarf bulbs will flower for the first year at least in shade, even though they may not persist there.

VARIEGATED AND GOLD-FOLIAGED PLANTS THAT TOLERATE SHADE

SHRUBS AND TREES

Acer palmatum—several varieties

Arundinaria viridistriata (bamboo)
Aucuba japonica vars.
Azara integrifolia 'Variegata'
A. microphylla 'Variegata'
Berberis × *stenophylla* 'Pink Pearl'
Buxus sempervirens 'Argentea' &
'Aureovariegata'
Camellia × *williamsii* 'Golden
Spangles'
Cleyera fortunei
Cornus controversa 'Variegata'
C. nuttallii 'Gold Spot'
Daphne odora 'Aureomarginata'
Fuchsia magellanica 'Variegata' &
'Versicolor'
Griselinia littoralis 'Dixon's Cream' &
'Variegata'
Hydrangea 'Tricolor'
Hypericum × *moseranum* 'Tricolor'
Ilex × *altaclarensis*—several varieties
Ilex aquifolium—several varieties
Kerria japonica 'Variegata'
Leucothoe fontanesiana 'Rainbow'
Ligustrum ovalifolium 'Argenteum'
& 'Aureum'
Lonicera nitida 'Baggesen's Gold'
Osmanthus heterophyllus 'Aureomar-
ginatus' & 'Variegatus'
Pachysandra terminalis 'Silveredge' &
'Variegata'
Pieris japonica 'Variegata'
Ribes sanguinea 'Brocklebankii'
Rubus idaeus 'Aurea'
Sambucus nigra 'Albovariegata' &
'Aurea'
Sambucus racemosa 'Plumosa Aurea'
Stachyurus chinensis 'Magpie'
Taxus baccata—several varieties
Ternstroemia gymnanthera 'Variegata'

Vinca major 'Variegata'
V. minor 'Variegata'
Weigelia japonica 'Variegata'
W. 'Looymansii Aurea'

CLIMBERS

Actinidia chinensis 'Variegata'
Euonymus fortunei radicans—several
varieties
Hedera spp.—several varieties
Lonicera japonica var. *halliana*
'Aureoreticulata'

HERBACEOUS PLANTS

Ajuga reptans 'Variegata' & 'Multi-
color'
Arum italicum 'Pictum'
Brunnera macrophylla 'Variegata'
Convallaria majalis 'Variegata'
Cyclamen spp.
Filipendula ulmaria 'Aurea'
Geranium macrorrhizum 'Variegata'
Hosta—several varieties
Iris foetidissima 'Variegata'
Lamium galeobdolon 'Variegata'
L. maculatum 'Aureum'
Lunaria biennis 'Variegata'
Luzula maxima 'Variegata'
Lysimachia nummularia 'Aurea'
Milium effusum 'Aureum'
Miscanthus sinensis 'Variegatus' &
'Zebrinus'
Molinia caerulea 'Variegata'
Phalaris arundinacea 'Picta'
Polygonatum japonicum 'Variegatum'
P. multiflorum 'Variegatum'
Pulmonaria saccharata 'Argentea'
Saxifraga umbrosa 'Variegata'

Index of Plants

When there is more than one page reference, main entries are in *italics*.
Illustrations are indicated by **bold** figures.